LOCAL ECOLOGIES

fulcrum

UMass Boston

CVPA
COLLEGE OF VISUAL AND PERFORMING ARTS
UMass Dartmouth

UMASS LOWELL

Collective Futures Fund

Dresher Center FOR THE HUMANITIES

UMBC

CCI
CLIMATE CHANGE INITIATIVE
University of Massachusetts Lowell

LOCAL ECOLOGIES

ARTISTIC INVESTIGATIONS OF EASTERN MASSACHUSETTS

KIRSTEN SWENSON
REBECCA UCHILL

Amherst College Press

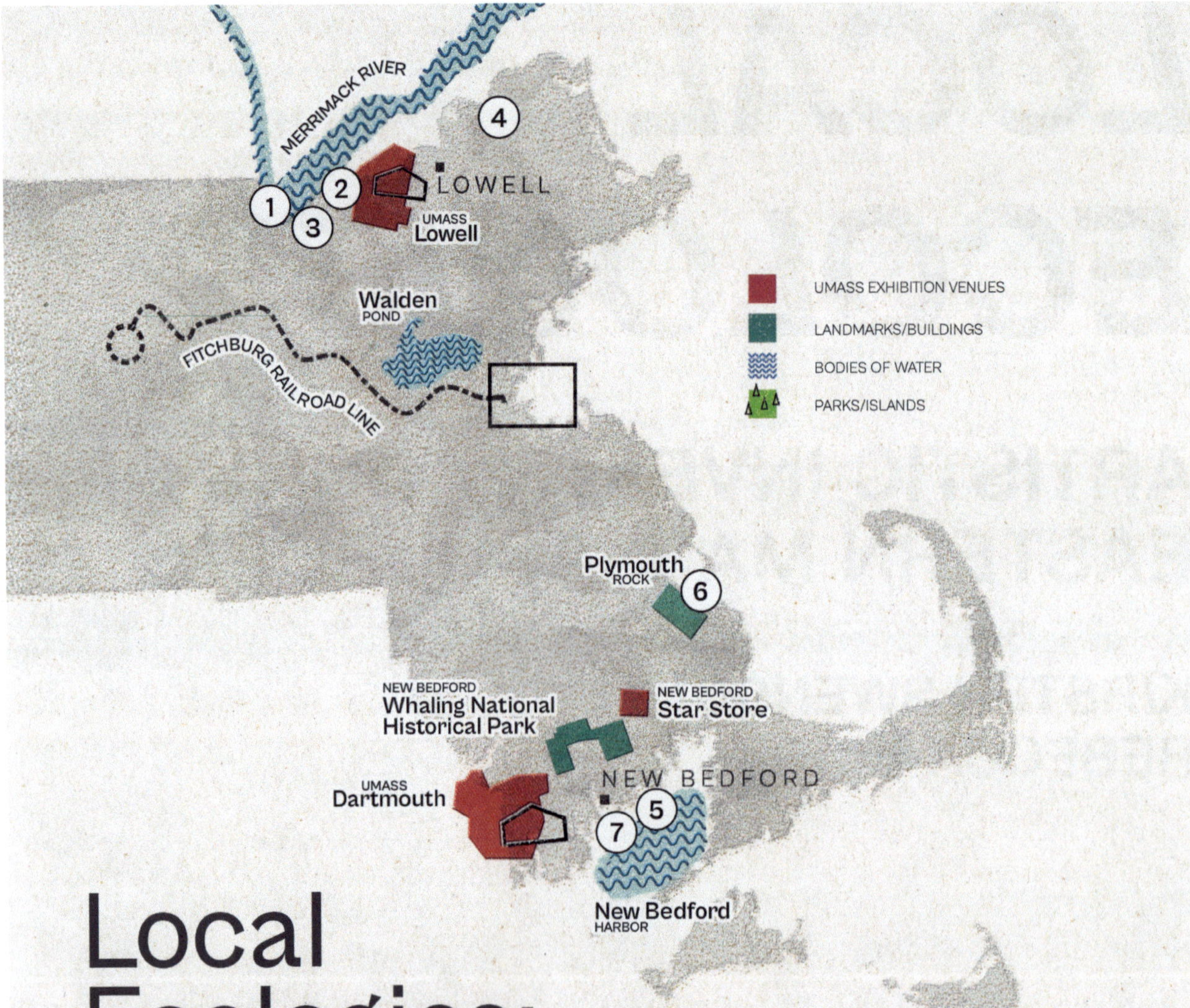

Local Ecologies:

Artistic Investigations of Eastern Massachusetts

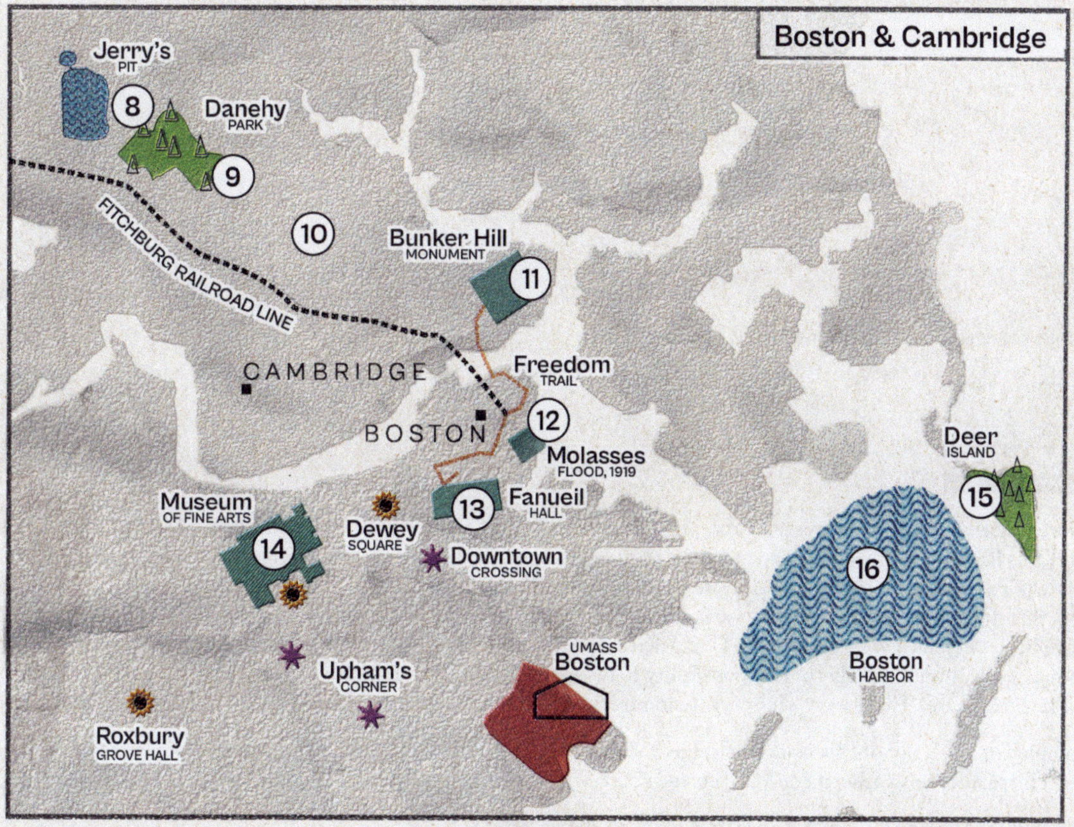

1. The Mouth: A Merrimack River Project, EVELYN RYDZ
2. Waste Knot, Want Knot, ANDREW S. YANG
3. Vân Hà (Cloud River), DUY HOÀNG
4. Clean River Project, ROCKY MORRISON
5. Dear Harbor Radio, PLOTFORM (JANE D. MARSCHING + ANDI SUTTON)
6. Mineral Spirits, DAN BORELLI
7. The Whiteness of the Whale and New Bedford's Superfund Site, DAN BORELLI
8. Color Fields, DAN BORELLI
9. Turnaround/Surround, MIERLE LADERMAN UKELES
10. Looking for a Landscape, MATTHEW MAZZOTTA
11. Bunker Hill Monument Projection, KRZYSZTOF WODICZKO
12. 19/19 Molasses Intervals, MARÍA MAGDALENA CAMPOS-PONS
13. Auction Block Memorial at Faneuil Hall, STEVE LOCKE
14. Horseshoe Crab Garden for Raven Reshapes Boston: A Native Corn Garden at the MFA, ELIZABETH JAMES-PERRY (Aquinnah Wampanoag)
15. Ecologies of Acknowledgment, SARAH KANOUSE AND NICHOLAS BROWN
16. Indigenous Boston Harbor Tours, NICHOLAS BROWN, FARIES GRAY (Massachusett), NIA HOLLEY (Nipmuc), SARAH KANOUSE, ELIZABETH SOLOMON (Massachusett)

✱ Dance Courts (Downtown Crossing and Mary Hannon Park and Strand Theatre, Upham's Corner), ds4si—DESIGN STUDIO FOR SOCIAL INTERVENTION

✿ Roxbury Sunflower Project (GROVE HALL), EKUA HOLMES, Radiant Community, Roxbury Sunflower Project (THE MFA), EKUA HOLMES, Seeds of Love and Justice, Roxbury Sunflower Project (DEWEY SQ.), EKUA HOLMES

The complete manuscript of this work was subjected to a partly closed ("single-anonymous") review process. For more information, visit https://acpress.amherst.edu/peerreview/.

Published in the United States of America by Amherst College Press

Manufactured in the United States of America

Library of Congress Control Number: 2025949114

DOI: https://doi.org/10.3998/mpub.13189112

979-8-89506-027-8 (paperback)
979-8-89506-029-2 (hardcover)
979-8-89506-028-5 (open access)

Cover image: Andrew S. Yang, *Plasticene Nest,* detail from *Waste Knot, Want Knot*, 2019.

Map: Padmini Chandrasekaran, *Local Ecologies Map*, 2025.

Contents

Acknowledgments

We want to first acknowledge that this volume is being finalized for publication in a very different context from those in which it was initially conceived, and later written. When, in 2020, we proposed to reflect on the ideas and processes that created the 2018–2020 UMass-based series of research probes, public programming, and a traveling exhibition, all assembled under the title *Local Ecologies*, this seemed like an opportunity to consider the complex ecosystems of persons and processes that were defining history and culture in specific regional places, over a discrete series of recent years. The world quickly changed around us. Many of our associated videos were made during high pandemic times, as we learned how to use Zoom. Some of the monuments we wrote about initially ceased to exist in the same forms, or locations. As we assembled the multimedia assets for this project, we continued to update texts responsively until 2023. Now, following a lengthy period of asset and metadata processing, we are submitting this volume in April of 2025, and looking back at this small corner of time, space, and history is taking on new meanings. Around us, institutions of history, culture, and education are being aggressively threatened and dismantled. Programs that champion diverse positionalities and histories, and accessible educational opportunities, are losing their personnel, buildings, and access to data/archives, and are being accused of "corrosive" or "improper" ideology.[1] We offer the texts, images, videos, sound pieces, artist books, maps, and other materials associated with this publication as an imperfect and incomplete archive from a brief but significant place and period of cultural discourse, and reckoning. We acknowledge that there are no absolutes in history, and hope that this volume will serve as a polyvocal, and at times, even contradictory, account that will contribute to a nuanced historical record and future learning.

This was an enormous project with many important contributors. First and foremost, we want to thank the core group of artists and curators who contributed to the original Local Ecologies exhibition: Sam Toabe, co-curator of the exhibition, and the core artists Dan Borelli, María Magdalena Campos-Pons, Duy Hoàng, Sarah Kanouse, and Nicholas Brown, Plotform (Jane Marsching and Andi Sutton), Matthew Mazzotta, Evelyn Rydz, and Andrew S. Yang. We also thank the expanded collaborators on the exhibition, including Gallery Directors Viera Levitt and Deborah Santoro, Graphic Designer Padmini Chandrasekaran, as well as exhibition and project contributors Chris Sweeney (UMass Boston), Shingo Furukawa (UMass Dartmouth), and Jean-Luc Alexandre (UMass Lowell). We thank program and project contributors Peter Galison, Rocky Morrison, Faries Gray, Caroline Jones, Roger Mandle, Misha Rabinovich, Juliette Rooney-Varga, Andy Schnetzer, and Elizabeth

Solomon. We also acknowledge key institutional partners including New Bedford Whaling National Historical Park; UMass Boston Marine Operations; the Providence Biennial for Contemporary Art; AHA New Bedford; and "ReSeeding the City: Ethnobotany in the Urban" at Brown University. We also thank our UMass institutional leaders who supported this work. These include David Klamen, Laura Franz, A. Lawrence Jenkens, Matthew Roy, Anna Dempsey, Luis M. Falcón, Joseph Hartman, Sue Kim, Stephen Mishol, and Ellen Wetmore.

When the exhibition was converted into a book, we worked closely with a number of project contributors and assistants, including students, on various elements of its multimedia production. These include: Felicia Bornstein, Heather Holmes, J. Engels, Jaslyn Tabourne, Libby McGrosky, and Gina Pantalone. Daniel Bazarian and Wednesday Klevisha assisted with video production. We are grateful to Amor Campos, Joëlle Fontaine, and Raquel Friedman Vargas for image assistance. We thank Katie Rokakis for her production assistance and coordination. And we are especially grateful to Lauren Berlin, Assistant Editor and Media Asset Manager, who brought this project to the finish line.

A number of funding sources helped this work become materialized in programs, conversations, artist books, exhibitions, all manner of material culture, and excursions on boats, bikes, and buses, all of which are part of this volume in various ways. We are grateful for the support of:

University Hall Gallery, UMass Boston
The Paul Hayes Tucker Fund, UMass Boston
Office of the Dean, College of Visual and Performing Arts, UMass Dartmouth
Leduc Center for Civic Engagement, UMass Dartmouth
Research and Scholars Investment Fund, UMass Lowell
Open Educational Resources Grant, Office of the Provost, UMass Lowell
Department of Art & Design and College of Fine Arts, Humanities, and Social Sciences, UMass Lowell
National Park Service
Collective Futures Fund, part of the Regional Regranting Program of the Andy Warhol Foundation for the Visual Arts, administered by Tufts University Art Galleries
Mass Cultural Council
The Paul & Edith Babson Foundation, in dedication to Newell Flather
Dresher Center for the Humanities, UMBC

Finally, thank you to Hannah Brooks-Motl, for believing in this work, and sticking with this project through many years of pivots and disruptions, and to Sara Smith for making the original introduction.

Kirsten Swenson and Rebecca Uchill

Part I

On This Ground

CHAPTER 1

In the Absence of Cultural Reflections: Looking for a Landscape

In his 2009 artwork *Looking for a Landscape*, artist Matthew Mazzotta sets up a mobile utility box in the streets of Cambridge, Massachusetts, then unfolds it to reveal a pop-up viewing platform stocked with cushions and sets of binoculars, open for use by passersby. The short video, presenting the jerky stop-action movements of a jaunty engineer placing this surprising object in the middle of a city sidewalk, seems

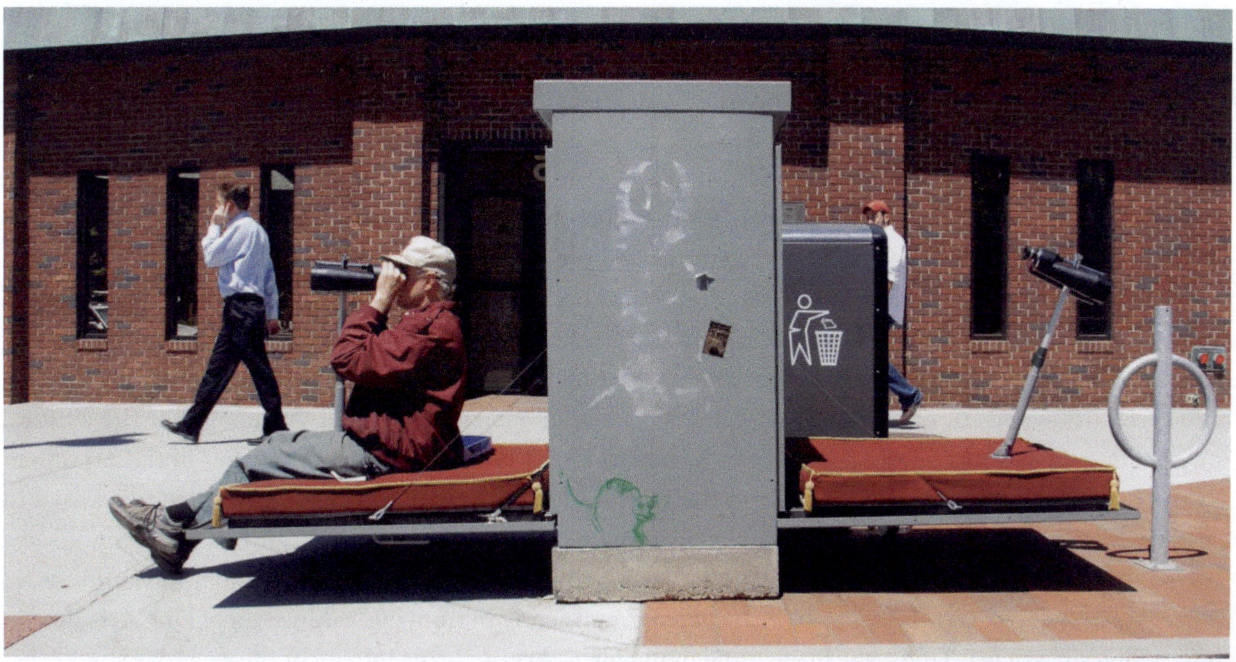

FIGURE 1.1 Image still from Matthew Mazzotta, *Looking for a Landscape*, 2014, https://doi.org/10.3998/mpub.13189112.cmp.2

both comedic and surreal: what vistas might be revealed from this strange and unexpected apparatus? We don't see the landscapes framed in the binocular lenses of our presumed-inadvertent tourists; we do see their facial expressions in longer still frames, smiling, or concentrated. The gesture of converting a piece of infrastructure and a stretch of city street into a scenic viewpoint has particular resonance in the touristic landscape of New England, for which Freedom Trail patriotism and transcendentalist landscapes have long been the subjects of travel industry branding and pervasive historical markers. This book is about looking for other regional landscapes and ecologies.

In this volume, we chronicle cross-sections of places in Eastern Massachusetts that were created by contemporary artists invited to participate in a series of programs and cycle of exhibitions between 2018 and 2020. The project, *Local Ecologies*, was shared by three UMass campuses—Boston, Dartmouth, and Lowell—and included interdisciplinary research commissions, community partnerships with local organizations, class offerings, workshops, new productions of artworks, public programs, performances, and numerous activities beyond the gallery walls. Each iteration of the exhibition changed responsively to the site in which it was presented—certain projects in and outside of the galleries were tied to specific localities (e.g., boat tours of the Harbor Islands, radio broadcasts about the New Bedford Harbor, and an art installation that used Merrimack River water as a material). The changing nature of this exhibition series reveals that the connotations of art and place are open-ended and relational in nature. Similarly, the book that follows not only documents the works from the *Local Ecologies* exhibition; it expands on these works with updated conversations, essays, reflections, expanded projects, and prompts for continuance.

In viewing Mazzota's video, one cannot help but note the low-lying vantage of his viewing platforms—the artist's modified utility device is hardly an elevated prospect or landscape overview. One imagines that through these binoculars the density of buildings and the crossings of close passersby would be presented as obstructions, hard to place into focus through the binoculars' magnified gaze. In this sense, "looking for a landscape" may point to that which has perhaps become too far away to see through the lenses we have been given—the landscapes that are obfuscated by the built environments that we inhabit, or the cultural stories they reinforce. As artist and ecologist Elizabeth James-Perry, a registered member of the Aquinnah Wampanoag nation, noted in connection to the multipart art installation *Garden for Boston* (discussed in Chapter 2), "It's very strange as a Native person in modern times to walk through Boston and not see a single reflection of myself or my culture."[1] Her work that participated in the installation, *Raven Reshapes Boston: A Native Corn Garden at the MFA*, installed prominently in front of the Museum of Fine Arts Boston in 2021, literalized a new landscape in view and living form. Art can bring into focus the everyday spaces that surround our travels, the striations of history that form our pathways, and new inroads to visions yet unseen. This volume brings together artists who do this work within the many, often contradictory, landscapes of New England.

When we began writing the texts for this volume in 2019, we saw colonial narratives as dominant regional histories presented in cultural environments of Massachusetts such as museums, parks, and wayfinding systems. Five transformational years later, in 2024, we much more commonly encounter the foundational stories of Indigenous experiences, the triangular trade, the industrial and labor histories of regional working mills and harbors, and other social and economic histories that have formed this place as profoundly as the American Revolution.

Lisa Lowe's theorization of transcontinental "intimacies" and modernity describes the "forcible encounters, removals, and entanglements omitted in liberal accounts of abolition, emancipation, and independence [by devising] other ways of reading so that we might understand the processes through which the forgetting of violent encounter is naturalized, both by the archive, and in the subsequent narrative histories."[2] The specificity of Eastern Massachusetts as site in the art and other works considered in the pages that follow (and digital assets that associate) evidences how similar entanglements, omissions, and new readings may pervade one small corner of the colonial landscape. Artists advocate for stories that may otherwise be obstructed or left out of the narratives stewarded by institutions such as city governments, museums, universities, park services, and private corporations. The contributors to this volume ask critical questions of specific Eastern Massachusetts landscapes, producing research and artwork that can guide us through places and their histories through conceptual, sensorial, and participatory explorations that encourage us to develop new modes of seeing and thinking about places.

The following chapter, "Not Neutral Ground: Creative Landscapes of Eastern Massachusetts," is an expansive introduction to this volume that demonstrates our methodology through considerations of well-known and less-recognized sites. Subsequent chapters of this book present newly commissioned artworks originally realized in the context of *Local Ecologies,* a series of programs and cycle of exhibitions. In addition, new essays and video roundtables document and extend a long-form dialogue between collaborators who worked and thought together during the exhibition and its public programs. Each chapter can be engaged on its own, and readers will find that each of the evolving artworks proposes new possibilities for addressing our local landscapes and local ecologies. All of the media in this book is freely available to view and in some cases download from the book's home page on the Amherst College Press website (https://doi.org/10.3998/mpub.13189112). We hope that the materials included herein will serve as models for readers to creatively and critically "look for" local landscapes and the constitutive entanglements that (in)form them.

CHAPTER 2

Not Neutral Ground: Creative Landscapes of Eastern Massachusetts

Of the hundreds (if not thousands!) of picturesque ponds in Eastern Massachusetts, we open with two of distinct geological origin and cultural significance: Jerry's Pond, on the land known as Cambridge, and Walden Pond, in the nearby town that we call Concord. One pond, dug in the mid-nineteenth century in the course of clay mining, is today fenced off and inaccessible though it sits within a densely populated urban environment. The other, a kettle pond formed by glaciers some 10,000 years ago, is a famous transcendentalist emblem of nature and refuge from a technologized world. Today, access to Jerry's Pond is prohibited by a chain-link fence, while access to Walden Pond is controlled less visibly through lack of public transportation and an \$8 parking fee (rising to \$30 for out of state visitors). How have the epistemes of the nineteenth century continued their grasp into the twenty-first? How have visitors and residents claimed these spaces in ways that are different from how they are controlled by private and public managers? This chapter introduces concepts and histories formative for this volume as a whole, and looks at a number of contemporary artists who examine the histories and methodologies that define familiar--and less familiar—spaces, proposing new modes of legibility and claiming new stakes. Some of the artists discussed here were also contributors to the *Local Ecologies* exhibition and series of programs chronicled in the latter part of this volume. We begin with stories of two ponds local to Boston, and their salient cultural histories and variety of artistic responses. We then look at other artistic engagements with New England histories--canonical and otherwise--through interventions in, and creations of, works on the scale of monuments, counter monuments, new landscapes, and other built environments. This overview sets the context for the revisitation of *Local Ecologies* that follows.

JERRY'S POND

The possessive "Jerry's Pond" establishes the land claim of Irish-born brick-worker and clay pit owner Jeremiah McCrehan.[1] For much of its existence Jerry's Pond has also been known as Jerry's Pit in reference to the clay extracted from this site. Jerry's Pond is surrounded by dense vegetation and teems with plant and animal life, a wild refuge that has been fenced off from sanctioned human activity for some sixty years. This unlandscaped space is contained within a border surrounded by a highly organized system of sidewalks, bike trails, and parking lots. It is abutted by a recreation area with playing fields and a public pool, as well as Alewife Station, a busy transit hub that is the terminus of the Massachusetts Bay Transportation Authority (MBTA) Red Line on the border of Cambridge and Arlington. The high-rise Rindge Towers with nearly 800 subsidized units are across the street (two of the towers have been named the Fresh Pond Apartments, in reference to another pond that lies across a busy thoroughfare). The nine-acre site is encircled by a high chain-link fence.

A years-long attempt to reclaim and render legible this inaccessible site is a story of a place yearning to be reconnected to its social surrounds. Artist Dan Borelli's 2019 public art proposal *Bric-à-Brac: A Collaborative Brick-Making Project for Jerry's Pit* began with a consideration of the area's history of clay extraction and large brickmaking industry. Borelli initially proposed to collaborate with residents of the Rindge Towers and Jefferson Park (another affordable housing complex) to create new brick designs for pathways that would connect neighborhood inhabitants to the site, and the past to the present. Using a direct observation spatial analysis strategy called "ground truthing," Borelli described the intentions in his proposal:

> *Today, this area bears subtle traces of the immigrant laborers and ecology that once defined this landscape. By collaboratively making bricks, especially with the nearby affordable housing residents, we'll be placing this object of construction in the hands of the residents so they can annotate, leave their marks, and then help us place their creations into the built environment surrounding their homes.*[2]

Borelli, whose work is examined in greater detail elsewhere in this volume, intended to catalyze a more participatory ownership of this salient place. His initial proposal has since evolved into a revised vision with the title *Color Fields: A Pathway from Jerry's Pit to Mass Ave,* to be realized through the Cambridge Arts Council as a Percent-for-Art project as part of the redevelopment of Linear Park.[3] The collaborative design of brick has been removed from the proposal for accessibility and maintenance reasons. However, the use of red brick continues in the new vision as a "counterpoint to the popular Freedom Trail, which uses red bricks to highlight historical sites around Boston."[4] The project points to the ubiquitous stories of Boston's history, commemorated in colorful paving stones on well-traveled grounds, as well as the possibility for other stories to become legible through new design approaches.

Boston and the other Eastern Massachusetts towns examined in this volume are rich with stories that are both framed and expanded through art and design activities. Environmental, social, political, and other histories thus weave together through cultural productions that inscribe experiences of place and constitute local identities, telling more nuanced, layered, and even resistant stories.

In 1865, Henry David Thoreau, a figure whose mythos has branded canonical regional identity, published his description of the Cape Cod shoreline as a "sort of neutral ground"—a place of "naked Nature" within the margins of wild seas (and, presumably, civilized nearby towns).[5] In *Local Ecologies*, which explores contemporary artistic investigations of place along Massachusetts waterways from Lowell to New Bedford, we propose that there is nothing neutral about this ground, nor about the premises of Nature or place, categorically. We compare divergent, sometimes contradictory, artistic interpretations of places and celebrate artists, designers, and other cultural producers who often tell multiple stories at once, while at the same time forging new ones.

Borelli's revised project is in development at the time of this writing, but in recent years other community-generated projects have asserted themselves within the visual landscape of Jerry's Pond. While a chain-link border and "PRIVATE PROPERTY NO TRESPASSING" signs discourage passersby from looking and

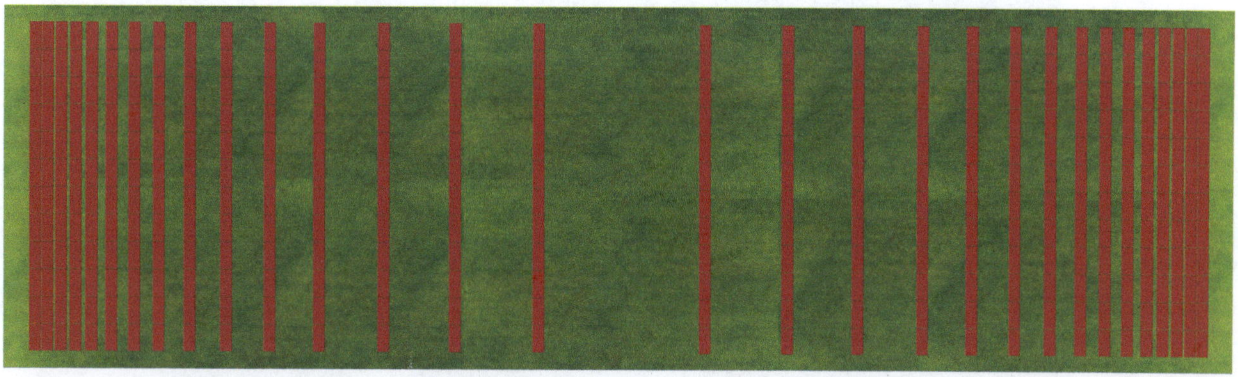

FIGURE 2.1 Dan Borelli, *DESIGN as Pattern + Pathway / COLOR FIELD*, from "Color Fields: A Pathway from Jerry's Pit to Mass Ave" proposal, updated 2023. Illustration of interlacing red bricks with green grass. Green area is 34' w x 10' h consisting of twenty-eight rows of twelve bricks per row totaling 336 bricks

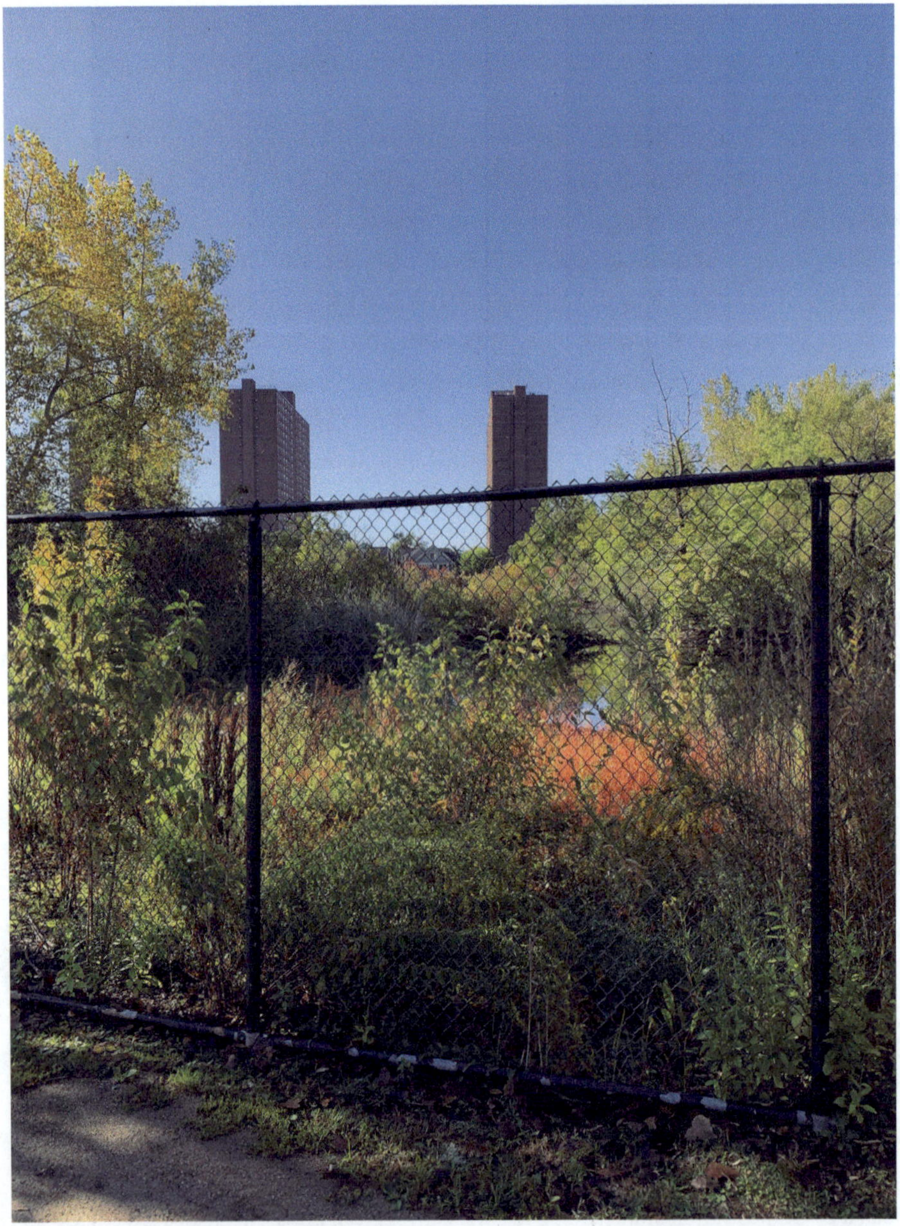

FIGURE 2.2 Fresh Pond Apartments viewed from Jerry's Pond. Photo: Dan Borelli

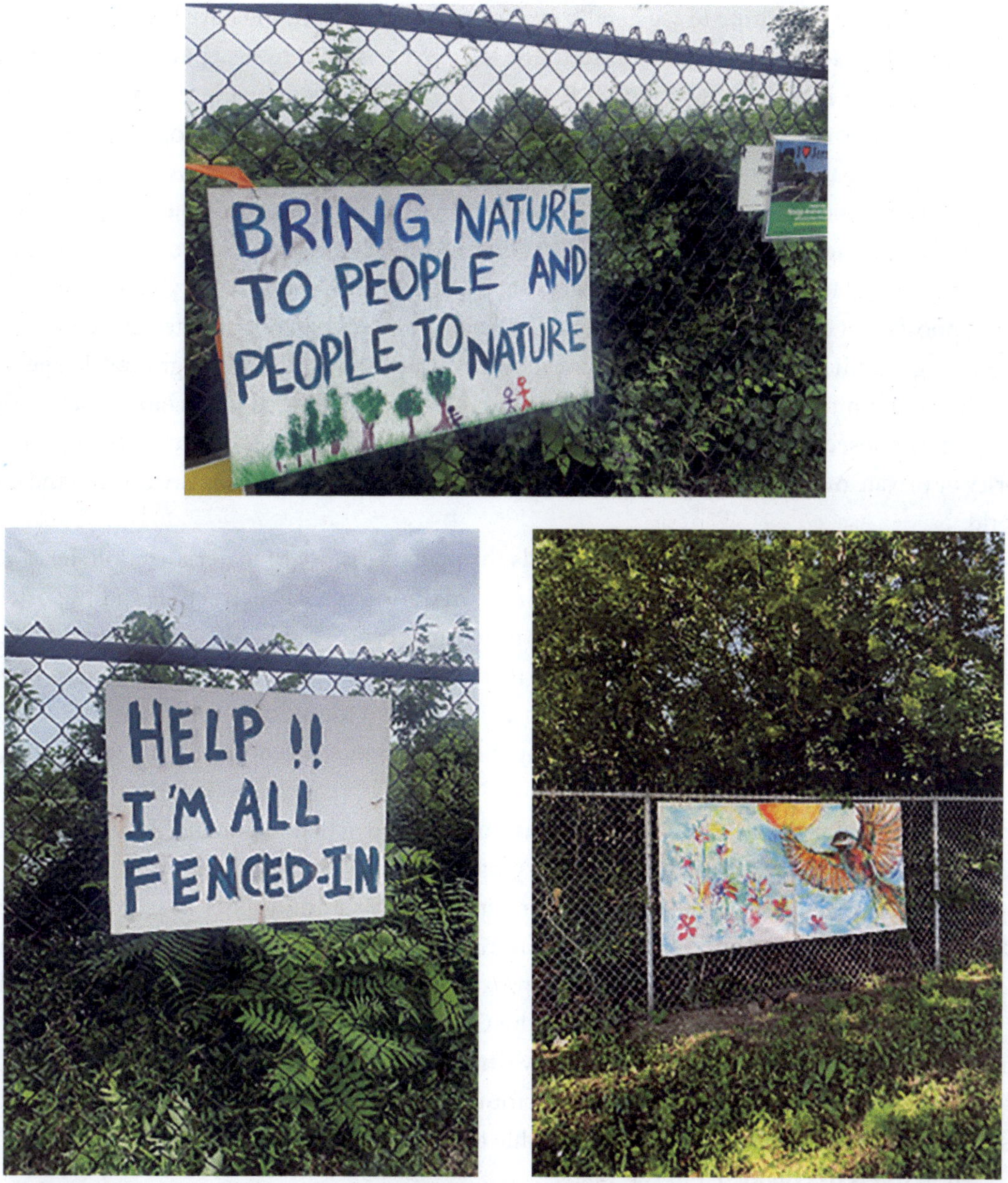

FIGURE 2.3 Community-created signage posted on chain-link fence around Jerry's Pond, documented in 2020. Photo: Kirsten Swenson

engaging with this place ("Nothing to see here!") such signals to keep walking have been answered by visible calls for attention. Hand-scrawled signs affixed to the fence read "I want to be a park when I grow up!" and "BRING NATURE TO PEOPLE AND PEOPLE TO NATURE." Elsewhere, a large painting hangs on the fence that depicts a soaring bird, flowers in bloom, a cloudless blue sky—a pictorial open space that responds to the chain-link enclosure with a visual language of access and cheerful vitality. Another artwork on site, identified with a sign reading "Signs of Life @ Jerry's Pond: A Community Art Project," is a grouping of directional signs indicating plant and animal species (Queen Anne's lace, mariposa, polilla) and points beyond (the future, the moon, Mogadishu). One sign notes that there are herons both at Jerry's Pond and in Ethiopia. These are signposts that converge extensive natural and cultural worlds in one situated cluster. Nearby, other hand-lettered signs indicate that native plant meadows are growing and implore groundskeepers "Do not mow!" These community-generated signs make visible the vibrancy of a complex biocultural ecology residing within the imposed boundaries of the chain-link fence. These responses challenge the very notion that an authority or private owner can sequester the pond: the pond, and its ecosystem, are diverse and connected to the world.

The site is also connected to its worldly surrounds through its history of materialization. Jerry's Pond, or "Jerry's Pit," is in many ways a vestige of the city's industrial history. Clay extraction and the brickmaking industry transformed the region's topography in the nineteenth century as brick companies mined deep clay beds, leaving vast pits in the landscape. Clay pulled from the beds north of Boston was used to make bricks to build mills, university halls, and houses. Pits such as Jerry's (and the aptly named Clay Pit Pond in nearby Belmont) were abandoned once clay was depleted by the mid-twentieth century, filling with water. Pits became ponds.

After Jerry's Pit was depleted of clay, the site was purchased by chemical maker Dewey and Almy and, in the 1920s, a chemical plant replaced the brick-drying sheds that were adjacent to the pit/pond.[6] In 1954, another chemical company, W.R. Grace, took ownership, and rubber and rubber-based products, including DAXAD (naphthalene sulphonate), construction materials, and asbestos brake-linings and insulation, were produced at the site.[7] Meanwhile the pond itself, proximal to crowded communities of immigrants and laborers in need of recreation space, was leased to the City of Cambridge by its corporate owners. A beach and bathhouse were built on one side, and for nearly fifty years, Jerry's Pond was a popular swimming hole. It was closed to the public in 1961, and a fence surrounded the site. Though records are incomplete, area residents have speculated that the site's closure was due to pollution: toxic levels of asbestos and naphthalene were detected in soil tests conducted in the 1980s.[8]

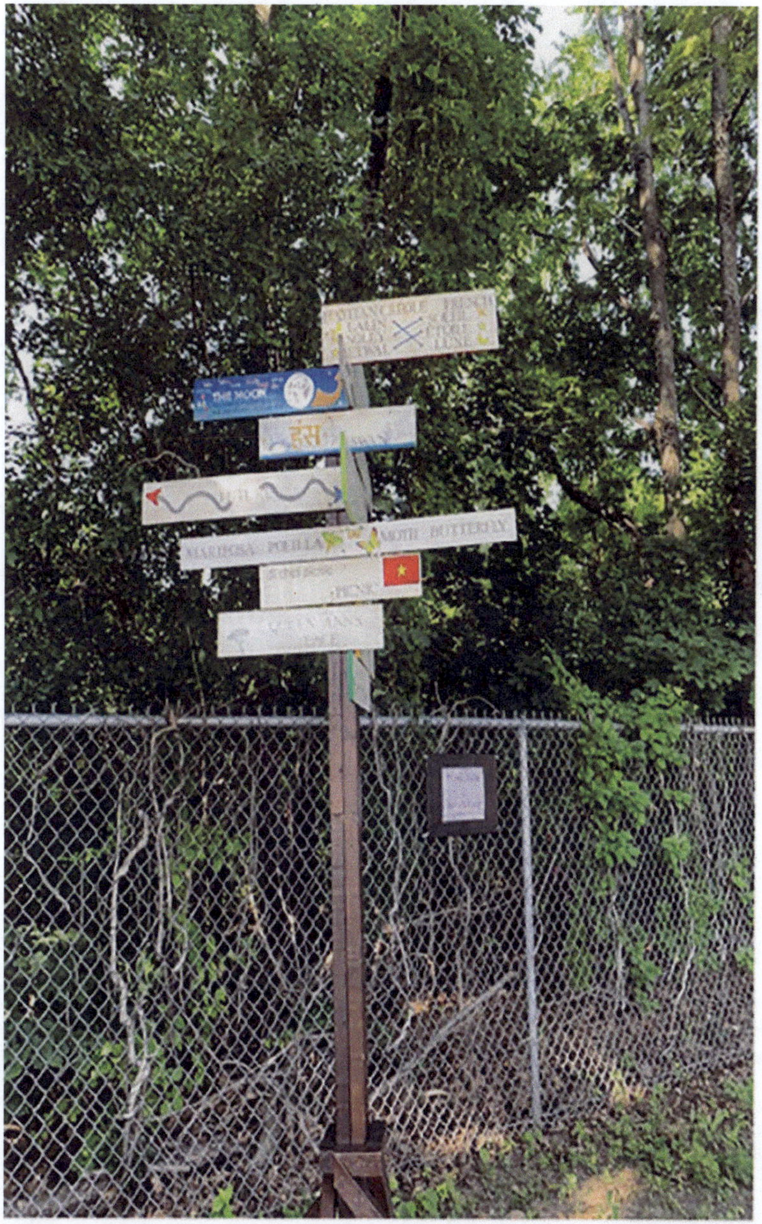

FIGURE 2.4 Encountering *Signs of Life @ Jerry's Pond: A Community Art Project*, 2020. Photo: Kirsten Swenson

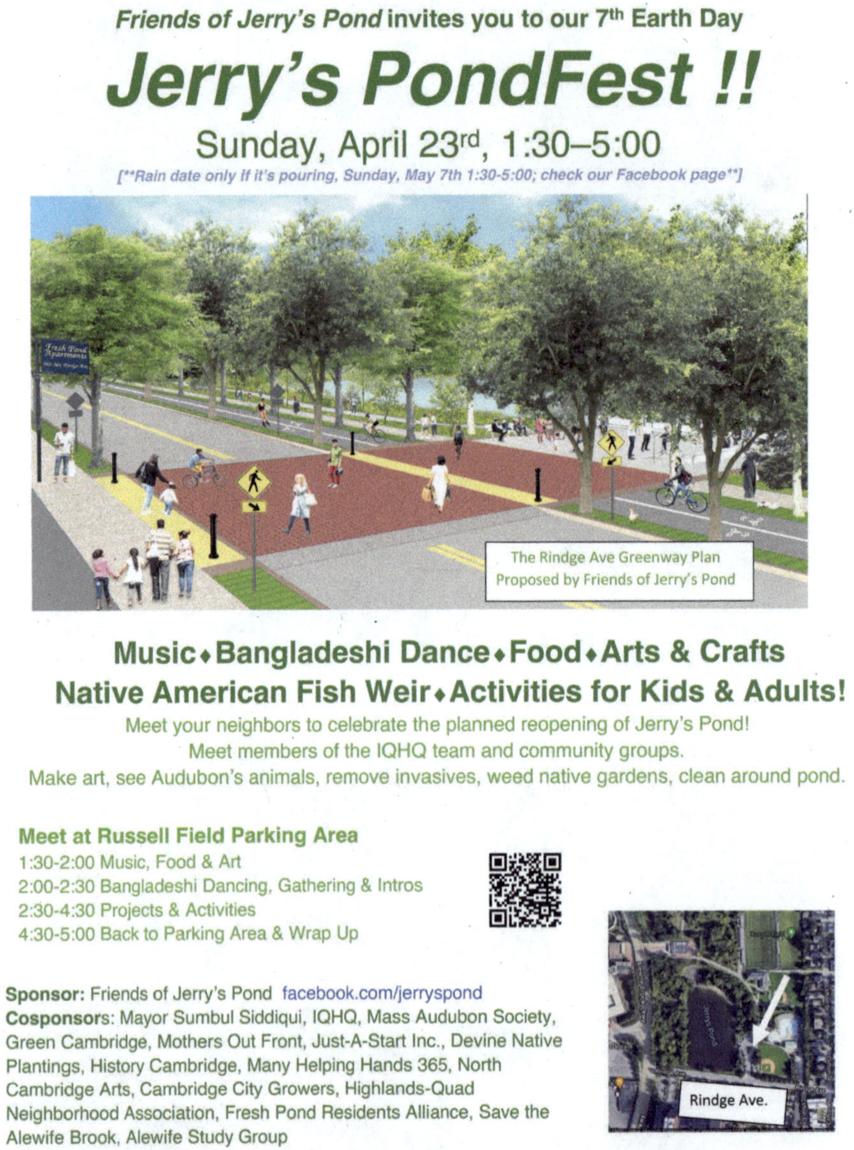

FIGURE 2.5 "Restore Jerry's Pond" community flyer, created by the Friends of Jerry's Pond, 2023

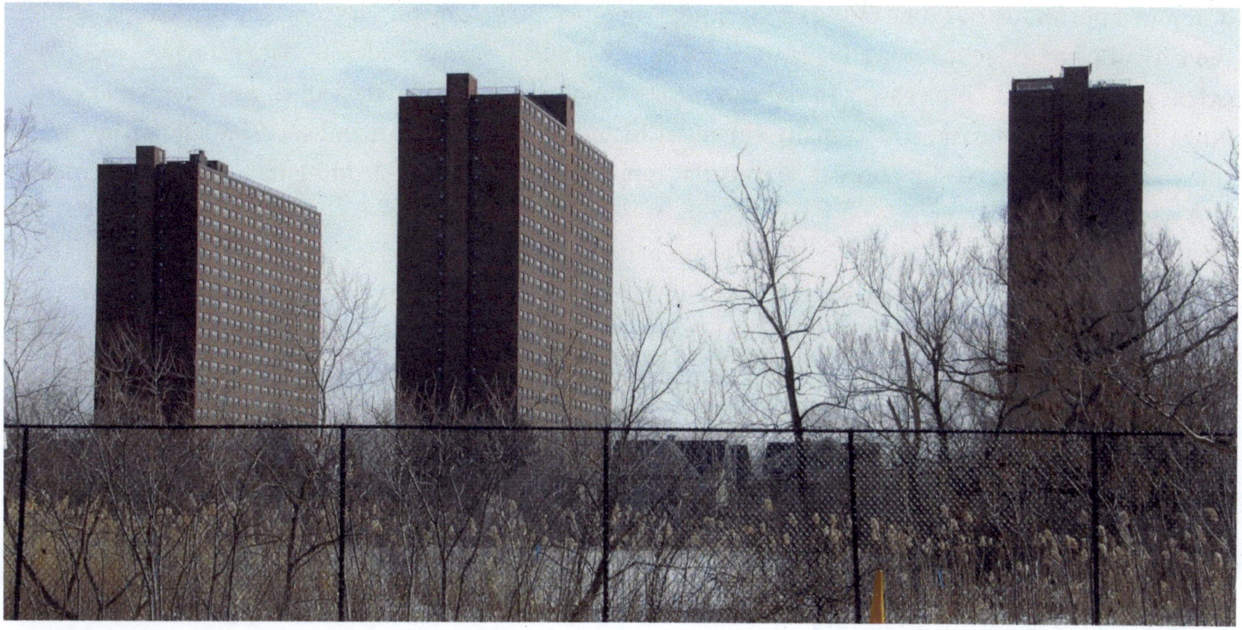

FIGURE 2.6 Rindge Towers, seen from the North

In 2020, Jerry's Pond again changed hands: it was part of a 26.5-acre plot purchased by IQHQ, a "life sciences real estate development company" that specializes in campuses for the biotech sector.[9] Jerry's Pond has not been remediated, and has remained off-limits to human activity since 1961, even as it is the closest potential green space for 4,000 low-income residents of the adjacent Rindge Towers. IQHQ has circulated renderings of an accessible pond and park with boardwalks and stated its intention to redevelop the site as a park, though community advocates are skeptical, questioning why the site's future should be determined by a private company rather than through a community process.[10] Indeed, Jerry's Pond is a poignant and visible symbol of conflicts between public rights to the city and privatization, and the perpetuation of environmental injustice.

On the opposite side of Rindge Towers from Jerry's Pond, other clay pits, on the site of present-day Danehy Park, had a different fate. The City of Cambridge repurposed these pits as a landfill when the New England Brick Company closed in the 1950s. The area north of the landfill was rezoned for high density public housing in 1965 in response to a need for low-income residences. Rindge Towers, built across a railroad track from the landfill in the late 1960s, concentrated lower income Cambridge residents on the edge of an active dump in a postindustrial zone of the city lacking amenities.[11] The clay pit served as the primary landfill for the City of Cambridge from the 1950s until 1972. The landfill was capped with backfill from the MBTA's extension of the Red Line subway in the early 1980s, and subsequently redeveloped as Danehy Park.[12] It is now the city's largest park, and its many amenities include a track, baseball and soccer fields, a playground, spray park, and wetlands that border a large, flat-topped hill popular for sledding in winter and picnicking and kite-flying in summer.[13]

In the 1990s, the landfill was redesigned by the artist Mierle Laderman Ukeles in collaboration with landscape architect John Kisseda to become a public earthwork: the resulting artwork, *Turnaround/Surround* (1989–ongoing) is a permanent, five-part "urban earth site."[14] Designed for the capped landfill and erstwhile clay pit, bordered by the Fitchburg Railroad, fragile wetlands, and the Rindge Towers, *Turnaround/Surround* manifests the artist's long investment in maintenance, remediation, and urban infrastructure in the form of a park that juxtaposes ecologies, sensory experiences, and social situations. Meandering paths encircling the landfill are made of "glassphalt"—asphalt that sparkles with crushed recycled glass from the community. "Smellers," abundant plantings of roses and lavender, conjure a reverse olfactory memory of the former dump "for those people who still have childhood memories of terrible odors," while "wavers" "accentuate the wind and open, free flowing landscape."[15] A wetland at the landfill's base is restored with cattails and marsh grasses.

The artwork encompasses "the path, plantings, events…experiences, fixtures—everything that makes up the total experience/journey," and is, by design, meant to be indistinguishable from the broader environment of Danehy Park itself, with no plaques designating "art."[16] Though many visitors may be unaware that they are experiencing a work of art, *Turnaround/Surround* is carefully designed as a place to consider ecological and social histories—to ask "Who are we? Where do we come from? What did we leave behind?"[17] This string of questions was a title Ukeles considered for the earthwork, summoning Gauguin's masterpiece *Where Do We Come From? What Are We? Where Are We Going?* (1897–8) hanging across the Charles River in the Museum of Fine Arts. Atop the landfill is a recycled rubber dance floor depicting the Milky Way. From here one can view the stars, or the Boston skyline, while dancing, playing, or seated on a massive sculptural "throne" of recycled aluminum. Ukeles extensively considered the "circular views"— "extraordinary views of Cambridge and Boston" reinforced by tree plantings that frame vistas.[18] The location of the dance floor and throne, on circular discs, encourage an embodied turnaround to take in the surround.

The view from Ukeles's *Turnaround/Surround* encompasses the diversity and range of a city and shows how complex access to sites like the one occupied by this artwork can be. On one side of the park, one-bedroom apartments are walkable to Whole Foods, Raytheon, and numerous biotech firms. On another

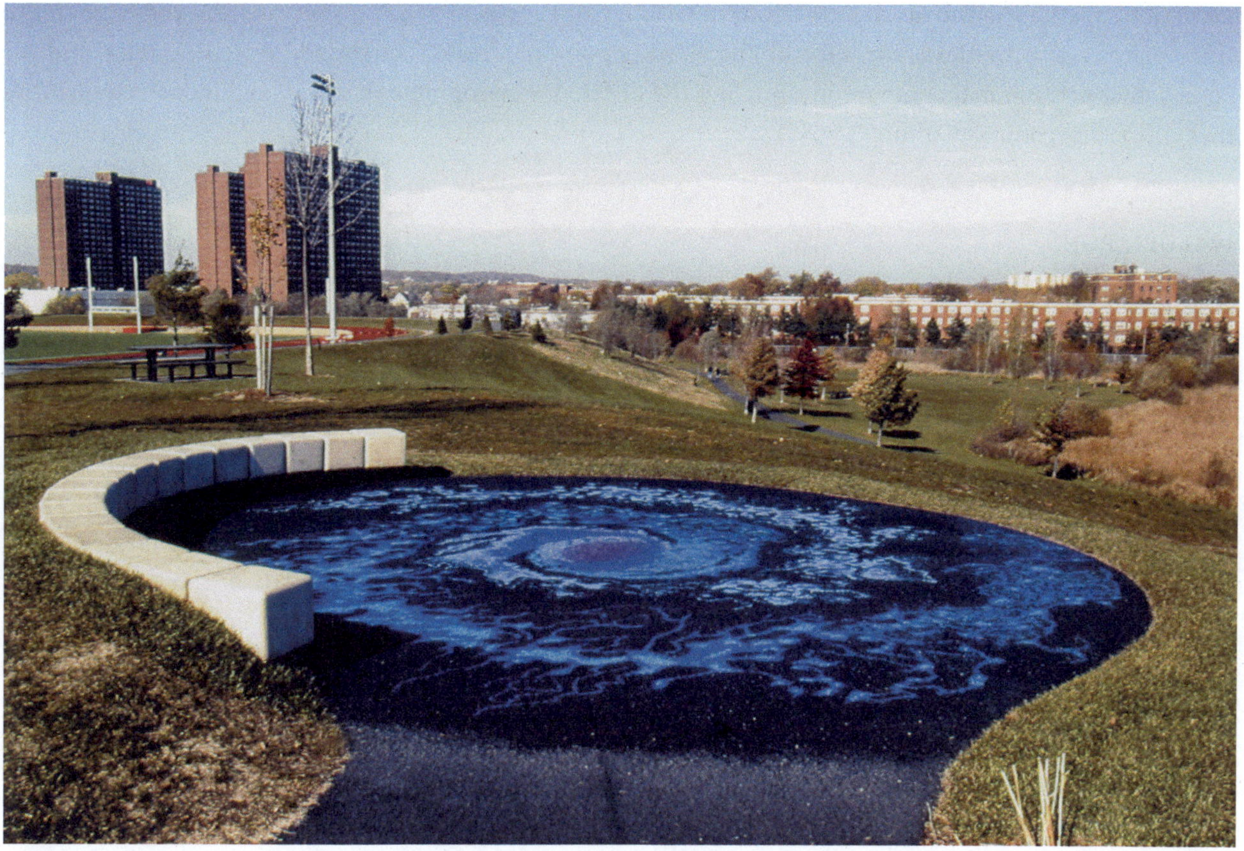

FIGURE 2.7 Mierle Laderman Ukeles, *Galaxy Dance Floor*, 2004. Part of the installation *Turnaround Surround* for Danehy Park, Cambridge, MA, 1989–ongoing, hand-placed rubber dance floor

side, residents of Rindge Towers adjacent to the inaccessible Jerry's Pond site are cut off from Danehy Park by active tracks of the MBTA commuter rail, once the Fitchburg Railroad, along the park's eastern border. City planners had sounded an alarm in 1990: "this situation [has] already caused a number of fatalities…Many residents, including young children and elderly people, cross the tracks to reach the Fresh Pond Shopping Center. Many more children will use this as a shortcut when…Danehy Park is completed."[19] Today, a high chain-link fence blocks access to the tracks, and there is no overpass—residents of the towers must walk a circuitous ¾ mile route to reach the park and Ukeles's *Turnaround/Surround*. Proximities in distance are negated by spatial alignments designated by ownership and access. The entanglements and convergences of these places and activities are framed by the viewing point of Ukeles' "surround." Borelli, Ukeles, and the community art sign makers share in signaling the different environmental, social, and industrial histories that define one common ground.

WALDEN POND

And now to our other pond. "The whistle of the locomotive penetrates my woods summer and winter, sounding like the scream of a hawk," wrote Henry David Thoreau of the Fitchburg Railroad that "touches the pond about a hundred rods south of where I dwell." He was, of course, referring to Walden Pond, a kettle pond about 20 miles northwest of Jerry's Pond. The Fitchburg line was built in the 1840s, connecting Charlestown and Cambridge to rural towns beyond, terminating in Fitchburg, a mill town and regional industrial center. The Fitchburg line passes strategically between Jerry's Pond and Danehy Park, former clay pits. The arrival of the Fitchburg Railroad had precipitated a Cambridge "clay rush" as fired bricks could be efficiently transported to build fireproof housing and mills in towns to the north and west.[20] Passenger cars, as well as freight cars carrying bricks made of clay from Cambridge clay pits, moved past Walden Pond, piercing the calm of Thoreau's woods and prompting him to reflect upon the railroad's effects on humanity. Wishing to live *deliberately*, "to front only the essential facts of life," Thoreau was unsettled by the railroad.[21] Nothing in the landscape represented the abstractions of technology and economic relations more than the railroad, a constant reminder to study the forest's precious "undisturbed solitude and stillness" and its chorus of chanting whippoorwills, trumping bullfrogs, and chirping squirrels. "We do not ride on the railroad; it rides upon us," Thoreau concluded bitterly. Thoreau's Walden was not entirely separate from the social and economic world from which he sought refuge.

Walden Pond may be the physical place most associated with nineteenth-century transcendentalist philosophies of the natural world that explored humans' place within the universe. For Thoreau, Walden was a place to answer the Emersonian call to "an original relation with the universe" amid a retrospective age.[22] The popular idea of Walden Pond as a natural retreat from society and dependence on a patch of earth is transposed onto a landscape, attracting half a million visitors each year.[23] In summer, the pond is a popular swimming hole that fills to capacity on hot days, leading to lines of cars waiting for the parking lot to reopen to the next carloads of visitors. Contamination from "pee and pesticides" periodically closes the pond to swimming.[24] That large visitor count hardly evokes the remote site of masculinist individualism that Thoreau mythology suggests.

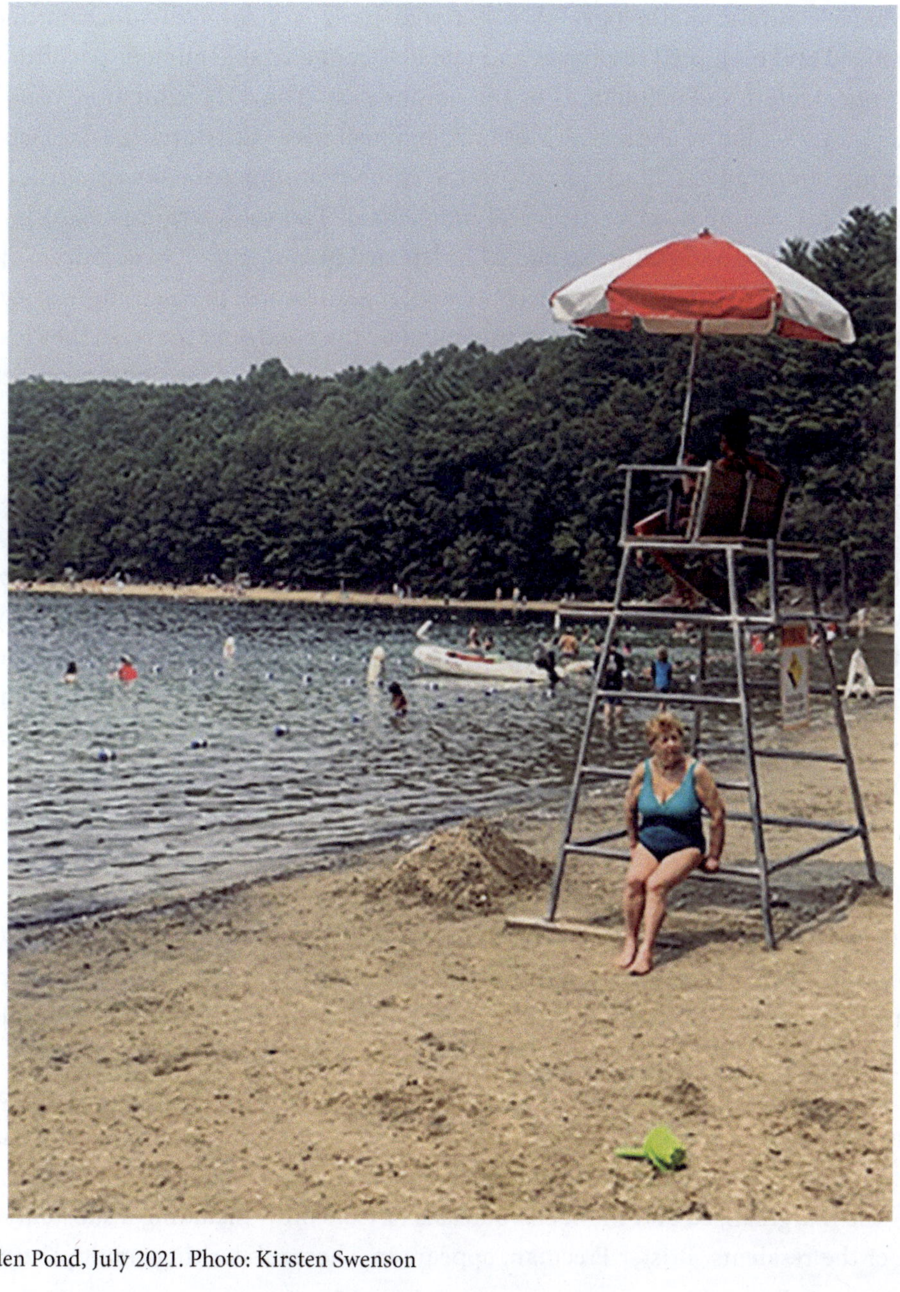

FIGURE 2.8 Walden Pond, July 2021. Photo: Kirsten Swenson

And yet, Walden's auratic mythology—as a notional sanctuary for individualism and autonomous living—has pervaded and prompted responses and updates from a sizable number of cultural productions, including contemporary art and exhibitions of the not-far past. The 2014 exhibition *Walden, revisited* at the nearby deCordova Sculpture Park and Museum, is illustrative. Curator Dina Deitsch described the exhibition's common imperatives: "Each project in the exhibition mines the fertile territory between real and idealized space, between distinctive historical moments of Thoreau's writing and today, and the ever-widening gap between nature and culture so narrowly depicted in *Walden*."[25] Oscar Palacio's photographs of Walden, for instance, home in on details of the contemporary landscape: the torn edges of signs once nailed to trees, the path markers guiding visitors to circumambulate the pond, and the trash they leave behind nestled in leafy underbrush. In Palacio's frame these details both untangle and join in transcendentalist calls for individuals to be attuned to their surrounding ecology.

Preluding *Walden, revisited*, another local exhibition, *Mildred's Lane/Renovating Walden*,[26] took form in a series of discursive and educational activities. The artist book/materials packet that accompanied the project contains the text "An Economist's Perspective on Walden" by Gilbert E. Metcalf, who comments on Thoreau's Walden experiment in terms of opportunity cost. "By living in a cabin in the woods outside of Concord for over two years, Thoreau could learn the true cost of living in a complex society. For living in society meant that Thoreau could not experience the solitude and time for reflection that he so eloquently describes in Walden."[27] Thoreau begins *Walden* with an account of "Economy" (the title of his first chapter) in which he meticulously details the financial expenses required to sustain his Walden life. Notably, where he does not pay in currency for a material, his accounting does not inventory a material cost. So, "two casks of lime" cost 2.43 ("that was high," Thoreau annotates), but other materials remain outside of this economic tally: ("the timber stones and sand…I claimed by squatter's right").[28] There is an implication that certain found materials (such as timber, or even land, when "claimed") are not a "cost" as they have not been purchased as commodities. But of course, resources do come from somewhere, as does the privilege of taking two years to perform this living experiment in the first place. The cost of Thoreau's own labor during this period also remains unquantified, as it also exists, for Thoreau, outside of conventional social and economic labor systems.

Walden is a shorthand for an imagined economy of an isolated act of "liv[ing] deliberately." Even so, during Thoreau's experiment the area was certainly not removed from a social matrix. In addition to the traversing of a train that "rode upon him," Thoreau's newly built home was in an area occupied by a sizable community of "the marginalized and the social outcasts of Concord," including a substantial Black demographic.[29] One of the residents, Brister Freeman, appears in Thoreau's writings multiple times, as tracked

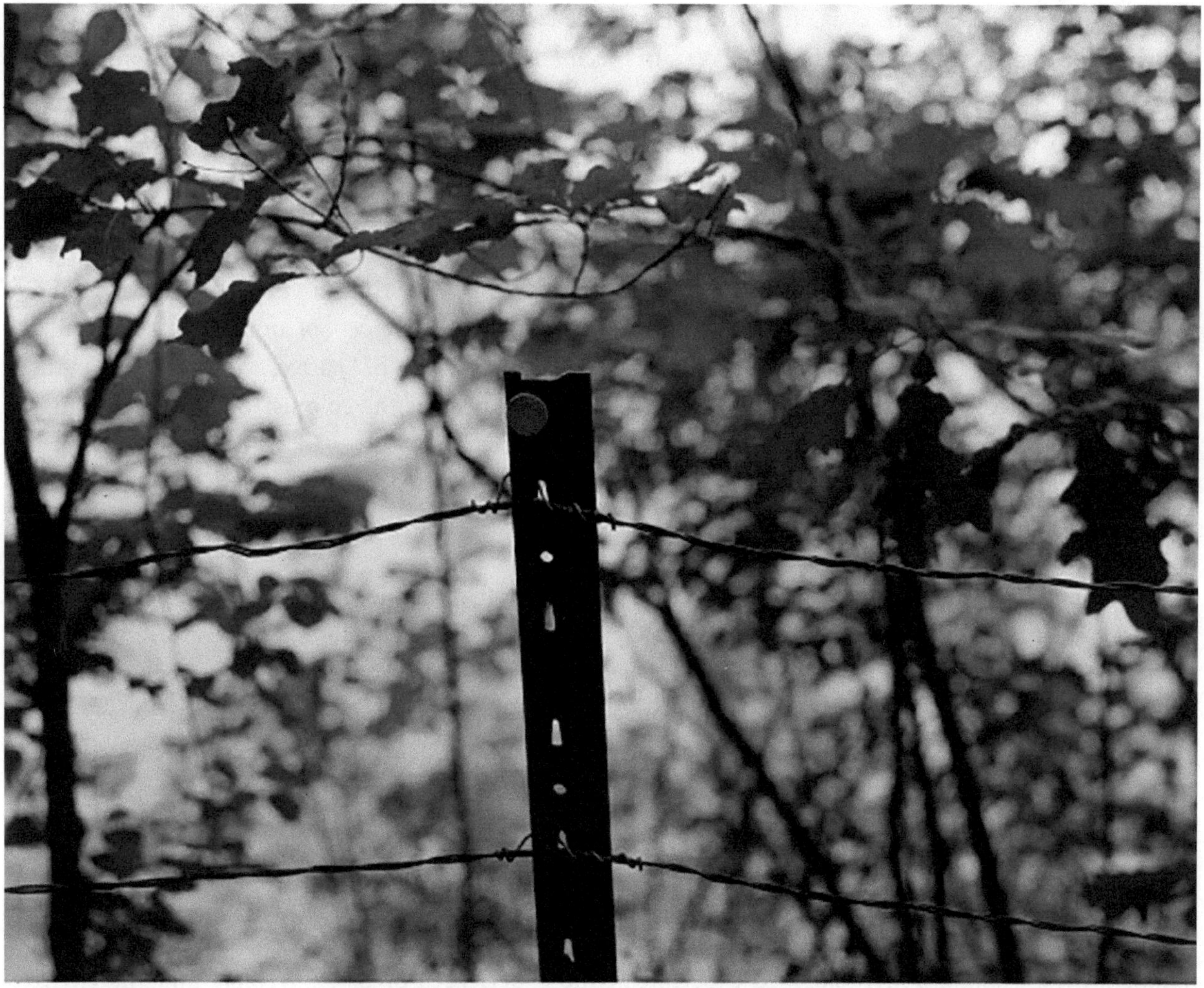

FIGURE 2.9 Oscar Palacio, Fence, 2014, from the series *Walden: Then and Now*

by Elise Lemire in *Black Walden.* In Thoreau's telling, Freeman is conflated with another local man, Sippio Brister; in his 1857 survey of Walden Woods, he notes that his property, "Brister Lot," had become "the state's because the owner, Brister, was a foreigner."[30] In 1791 Brister Freeman, a formerly enslaved man who also made his home in Walden Woods, was made to sign over his property to officials of Concord. This was nominally in response to his evasion of the poll tax, the same tax that Thoreau avoided paying in protest against slavery and the Mexican American War. In Freeman's case, this was a punitive act of disenfranchisement: losing his property made Freeman ineligible to participate in town meetings and local politics. These two men were contemporaries and neighbors sharing common spaces and navigating systems that produced distinct experiences with and relationships to their Walden land. Thoreau stayed at Walden during a two-year period from 1845 to 1847, roughly a century after the rough 1750 date to which cultural geographer William M. Denevan attributes the aesthetics of a national "pristine myth" of precolonial Americas.[31]

Even as we acknowledge the problems with the settler-colonial "pristine" mythos of New England and its links to manifest destiny land claims, we also acknowledge that the concept of an immobile and tethered "native" community (what Arjun Appadurai characterizes as an image of "natives...immobilized by their belonging to a place") is both reductive and false.[32] In that frame, it is the colonist, the anthropologist, or even the artist who ventures elsewhere, to the place being occupied or investigated, while Indigenous persons or ecologies can only flee or be subjected to the forces of these presumed-stronger interlocutors. The reality is much more complex. Appadurai acknowledges that:

> Most groups that anthropologists have studied have in some way been affected by the knowledge of other worlds, worlds about which they may have learned through migration trade, conquest, or indigenous narratives.... Even where contact with large-scale external forces has been, till recently, minimal, as with some Inuit populations, some populations in lowland South America, and many Australian aboriginal groups, these groups have constituted very complex "internal" mosaics of trade, marriage, conquest, and linguistic exchange, which suggests that no one grouping among them was ever truly incarcerated in a specific place and confined by a specific mode of thought.[33]

Just as in Lisa Lowe's intimate histories, discussed earlier, here we are again reminded that understanding place through its inhabiting societies is rarely (really never) a matter of a comparative intersection of monocultures. Thoreau's mythologized experiment, the experiences of Black Walden, and the environmental shifts of colonial conquest and industry are all part of the same networked systems of occupation, social and economic violence, and enmeshed relations between constituencies that in unison create place.

Seeing and rendering the interconnected stories of place is a form of critical design methodology and approach to ecosystemic thinking. In 1968, University of Pennsylvania landscape architecture students were, for the first time, instructed to draw and analyze a larger ecosystem (hydrological, geological, populational) rather than a discrete plot of land. Instructor Ian McHarg, known for his influential *Design with Nature* published in the subsequent year, led a studio in researching and mapping the full Delaware Upper Estuary; these maps were recently exhibited in the exhibition *Emerging Ecologies* at the Museum of Modern Art in New York (in a public Instagram post, artist Sarah Kanouse, whose work is included in this volume, queried the exhibition's overall tendency to "colonial eco-modernism"). In *Local Ecologies,* we seek a present methodology of cultural production and analysis that unbuilds and clarifies the complex and interconnected local topographies built by many contributors—this includes architects, scientists, colonists, developers, residents, artists, activists, neighbors, and many others. Walden is a place where essentialized notions of a landscape may have been inscribed in canonical writing, but it is also a place from which diverse human use and cultural production extend the vision of what environment is and can be. We welcome reconsiderations of Walden, the place, as well as *Walden,* the text, as culturally inscribed physical or textual monuments to transcendental heroics. Likewise, throughout this volume, familiar sites or historical events are estranged and re-produced through projects that undo essentialized narratives, while less familiar landscapes (akin to "Jerry's Pit") come into focus through cultural activations and productions.

NOT NEUTRAL: RESHAPING THE CITY

As we wrote this chapter during an extended pandemic lockdown, we saw critical interrogations of monumental objects and institutions in important cultural movements (Decolonize Museums, Black Lives Matter) as well as the physical dismantling of structures of colonialism in the removal of monuments across the country. Monuments are not innocuous, abstract symbols. In New England, they form a particularly dense proscenium of constructed structures and designated spaces and associating intended behaviors. Cultural historians have long understood the function of monuments as naturalizing the political, social, and economic histories they are determined to represent.[34] For obvious reasons, Christopher Columbus monuments—outright and explicit symbols of conquest—were among those that were brought under deserved scrutiny during an early 2020s cultural reckoning in the United States; the "beheading" of one Columbus monument in Boston was a swift, decisive rejection of the symbol as well as the cultural violence that it inscribes.

The violent implications of Boston's regional landscape of monuments have been crucially addressed through creative form by artists. For example, the verticality and relative permanence of a traditional monumental form such as the Bunker Hill Monument (1825), a 221-foot granite obelisk in Charlestown, Massachusetts commemorating the 1775 Battle of Bunker Hill within the war known as the "American Revolution," was made the corporeal substrate for Krzysztof Wodiczko's 1998 *Monument Projection.* Here, tragic contemporary stories of neighborhood violence were shared by Charlestown residents, animating a flat and opaque stone facade with the temporary projected stories of an embattled and grieving community. Wodiczko connects the brutality haunting this Charlestown community, a large public housing development that was encumbered by violence and the illness of drug addiction in the 1990s, with legacies of violence that built a nation. "The battle perhaps continues...for life, liberty, and pursuit of happiness," Wodiczko said of his *Bunker Hill Projection*, pointing to the lived experience of a neighborhood in the shadow of the famous monument.[35] Of course, the histories of violence that pervade this singular space hardly form a linear continuity. They are multifold, and represent material truths stacked upon material truths, all connected to a shared common ground.

Twenty years after the Bunker Hill projections, in 2018, artist Steve Locke proposed a more permanent rededication of the site of Boston's Faneuil Hall, built with wealth accumulated through enslaved labor and named for slave owner Peter Faneuil, who profited from the triangular trade. Locke's proposed *Auction Block Memorial at Faneuil Hall* was a bronze plaque proposed to be embedded in the ground along the Freedom Trail and across from Faneuil Hall, one of Boston's premier tourist attractions. The proposal contained the critical subtitle *A Site Dedicated to Those Enslaved Africans and African-Americans Whose Kidnapping and Sale Here Took Place and Whose Labor and Trafficking Through the Triangular Trade Financed the Building of Faneuil Hall.* The memorial would be inscribed with the route of the triangular trade: the same ships transported New England–produced rum to Africa, carried enslaved people to the Caribbean, and returned to New England ports laden with sugar produced on plantations.[36] Slavery persisted in Massachusetts until the 1780s, and many of New England's elite continued to accumulate wealth from enslaved labor in the Caribbean long after abolition.

This monument compels its viewers to recognize slavery as having been foundational for the region's economy. Locke's design embeds this history through establishing the "here" in the plaque as a site dedicated to this recognition, squarely a part of Faneuil Hall's history as Boston's colonial-era center of commerce. The horizontality of Locke's design—it is flush with the ground—and its incorporation of biological presence (the monument would be heated to 98.7 degrees, the temperature of the human body) would further integrate lived human experience within the landscape, making inseparable the ground itself, the enslaved laboring bodies, and the adjacent vertical Georgian facade inexorably connected to both.

Auction Block Memorial at Faneuil Hall reconceives the memorial landscape of New England. The design for *Auction Block* refuses standards of verticality, demanding a downward gaze to consider the ground itself as a locus of meaning rather than the abstract space of air. As Locke's description states, "I proposed an artwork to honor the actual and metaphorical space my ancestors occupied when they were brought here during the colonial period by Faneuil and men like him. I proposed my work in the service of those women

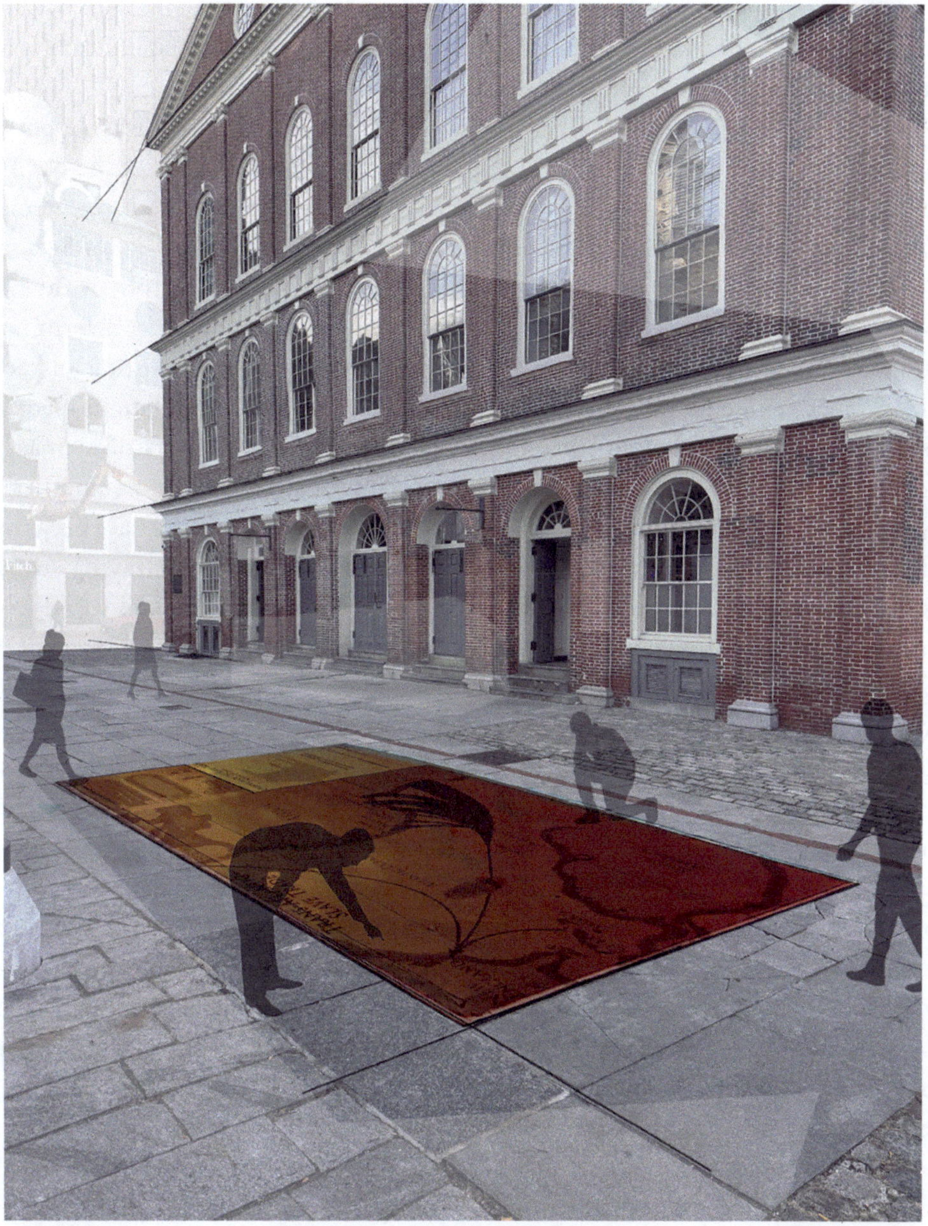

FIGURE 2.10 Steve Locke, Artist's rendering of *Auction Block Memorial at Faneuil Hall: A Site Dedicated to Those Enslaved Africans and African-Americans Whose Kidnapping and Sale Here Took Place and Whose Labor and Trafficking Through the Triangular Trade Financed the Building of Faneuil Hall*, 2018. Bronze with heating elements, 10 x 16 feet. Rendering by Julian Phillips © 2025 Steve Locke / Artists Rights Society (ARS), New York

and men who were stolen, sold, and worked to death. I proposed it to alter the Faneuil Hall marketplace into a site of contemplation of an atrocity against Black people."[37]

Auction Block Memorial at Faneuil Hall has not been realized. The proposal was supported by the City of Boston and the Boston Art Commission, but opposed by the Boston branch of the NAACP. As the organization communicated in an email to Locke, "The NAACP Boston Branch is centered on uplifting and advancing communities of color, with a focus on the Black community in the City of Boston. It is for that reason that we object to the installation of a slave auction block memorial in front of Faneuil Hall."[38] The NAACP did offer reasons for opposing Locke's memorial; their statement to Locke determines that *Auction Block Memorial at Faneuil Hall* would not be aligned with their mission of "uplifting and advancing communities of color."[39] Locke's memorial concept does not exalt or celebrate—this status is made manifest by its embeddedness. However, we also do not perceive this monument to be an example of "damage-centered" inquiry, as theorized by Eve Tuck, whose 2009 "Suspending Damage: A Letter to Communities" observes that "urban and Native, disenfranchised, overresearched but underseen" communities have been overwhelmingly subjected to research that "has historically been damage centered, intent on portraying our neighborhoods and tribes as defeated and broken."[40] Rather, Locke calls to account the built and social environments of the City of Boston for histories that may be embedded but not readily recollected in Faneuil Hall's touristic branding as a place to eat baked beans and clam chowder and celebrate a vague, ahistorical Revolutionary-era idea of Boston.

This project joins other recent actions by artists who have meaningfully inserted themselves into the contemporary landscape of memorials, calling attention to the specificity of place and blurring the lines of where monuments end and art begins. In 2019, artist Theaster Gates, working with Samaria Rice, relocated the Cleveland gazebo where Tamir Rice, a twelve-year-old Black child was killed by a white police officer named Timothy Loehmann in 2014. The gazebo had become a place of memorial and was planned for demolition by the city. Gates's Rebuild Foundation in Chicago became the new site for the gazebo structure. Art historian Sarah Lewis observes that the new placement is "in fact, an easement, a mound required by municipal zoning regulation to prevent drive-by shootings of the nearby residences. The structure associated with Rice's murder stands as a symbol of the interpenetration of the ground, land, and racialized life."[41] Here, an artistic act of relocation and dislocation reflects the site-specific context of memorial and the cultural assumptions that inhabit zoning ordinances. In 2020, video producers and activists Dustin Klein and Alex Cirqui projected texts and images of figures including George Floyd, Breonna Taylor, Harriet Tubman, and Frederick Douglass on a Richmond Virginia Robert E. Lee monument that had become a site of protest vigil and community gathering (the monument and base have been subsequently removed). This activity, begun

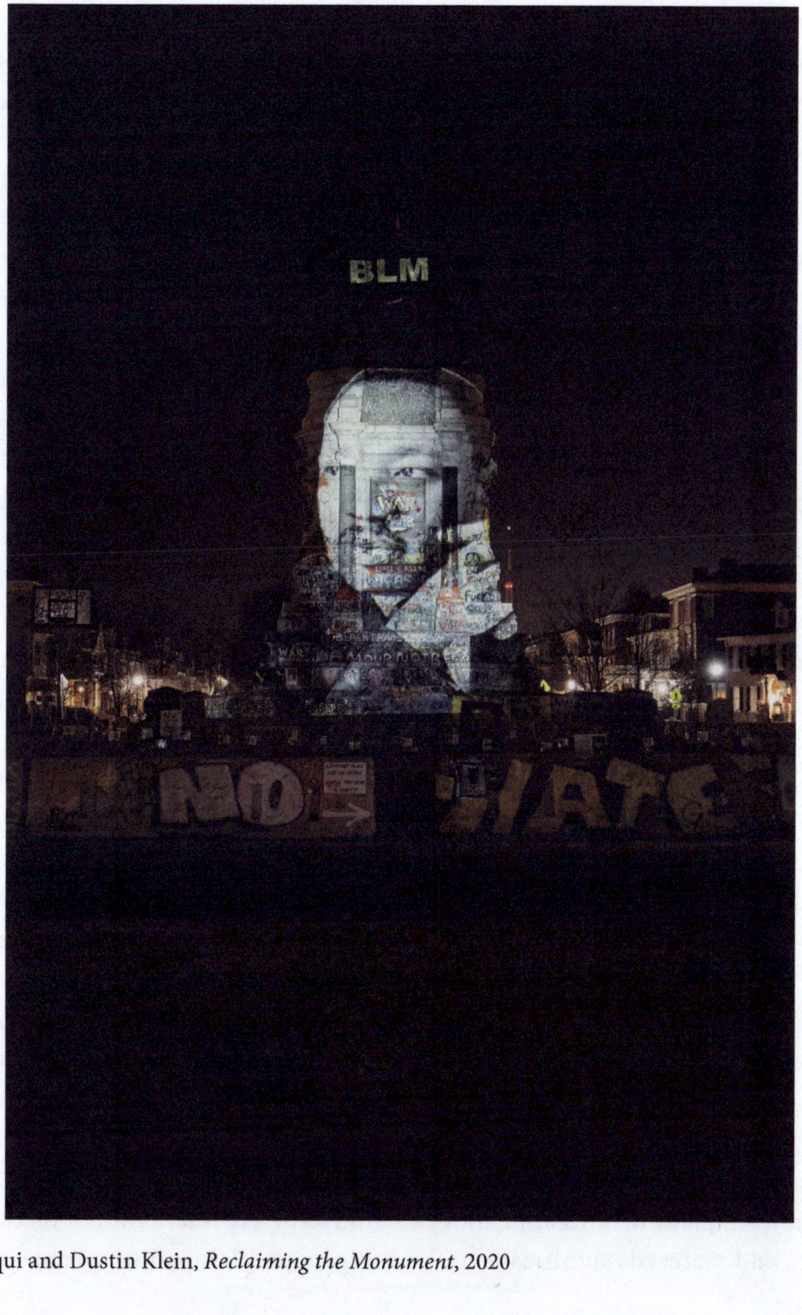

FIGURE 2.11 Alex Criqui and Dustin Klein, *Reclaiming the Monument*, 2020

as a nightly protest, was soon claimed by art world ambassadors. Critic Holland Cotter named this action among the "Most Important Moments in Art in 2020"; MoMA requested to include the project in their magazine. The producers reflected on how placing a title on the action for MoMA's publication changed their thinking about the project as art: "On some level it just gave us license to try and see where we could take it. Now it seemed like people were paying attention. We thought we were doing a protest thing.... The fact that this was shared so much on the internet and preserved in photographs gives it more of a long-lasting power [than a protest]...[and] makes it feel more like art."[42] The nomenclature and designation of art can provide a context for expanding radical acts of imagination and calling the attention of new audiences.

Ekua Holmes and Elizabeth James-Perry's *Garden for Boston* offered another approach to the intersections of art and memorialization, using cultivation to implant memory within a landscape. Holmes initially worked with sunflowers for her *Roxbury Sunflower Project* (2018), sponsored by Boston-based public art organization Now + There. Holmes invited community members—families, and civic organizations—to plant 20,000 sunflowers in Roxbury neighborhoods, including Grove Hall, throughout the summer of 2018. The sunflower is a native North American plant chosen by Holmes for its heliotropism and symbolism of hope and resilience. Roxbury, like other neighborhoods in American cities with predominantly Black and immigrant populations, has been underinvested—*The Boston Globe* characterized Roxbury of the 1980s as "a monument to racism and neglect."[43] But Holmes's celebratory sunflowers resist definition of place through inverse resources. Roxbury is a diverse center of the city of Boston, characterized by its close-knit communities, vibrant art and music culture, and a distinct geological bedrock conglomerate known as "Roxbury puddingstone." Holmes's plantings are an ornamental remaking of the environment that demonstrate a capacity to thrive. "This project is a seed of love for Roxbury, its geography, its historical struggles, victories over displacement, over being ignored," Holmes explains.[44] Holmes's later sunflower project in 2021, *Radiant Community*, staged a relationship between the humble, ebullient, resilient flower and the Museum of Fine Arts, a historically elite institution that has not always made all Bostonians feel welcome.[45] In 2022–2023, Holmes expanded her *Roxbury Sunflower Project* with a multiyear, multisite series of sunflower plantings with the title *Seeds of Wisdom*, presented throughout the public Greenway park in downtown Boston. The plantings are presented by the Public Art on the Greenway program as an "expansion of" the *Roxbury Sunflower Project*, illustrating how art, landscape, and nomenclature can draw associations between different places or neighborhoods within a city.

Elizabeth James-Perry's *Raven Reshapes Boston: A Native Corn Garden at the MFA* (2021) likewise deploys cultivation to implant historical memory and unsettle representational tactics. Her garden is a collection of plants and materials significant to the Indigenous Wampanoag people: native corn, beans,

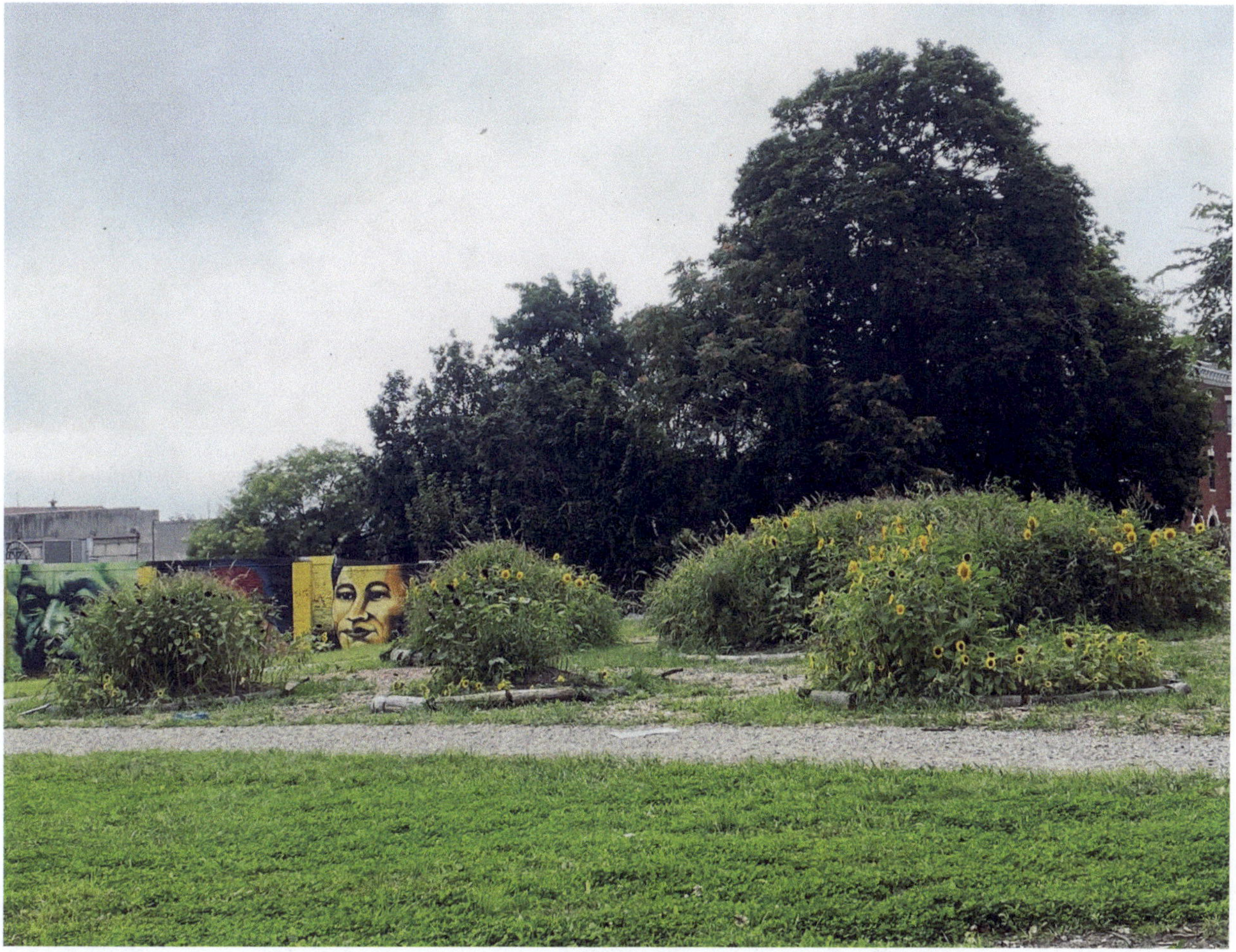

Figure 2.12 Ekua Holmes, *Roxbury Sunflower Project at Grove Hall*, 2024. Roxbury Sunflower Project/Ekua Holmes

and sedges planted in the shape of a horseshoe crab, surrounded by crushed quahog shells. James-Perry's garden is sited around Cyrus Dallin's *Appeal to the Great Spirit* (1909), a sculpture by a white artist that sentimentalizes Indigenous spirituality and has been in place at the museum's Huntington Avenue entrance since 1912. James-Perry emphasizes that her work is not a rebuttal to Dallin. In *The Boston Globe*, she was quoted saying "I was loathe, in my description, to even mention the Dallin. [The project] isn't

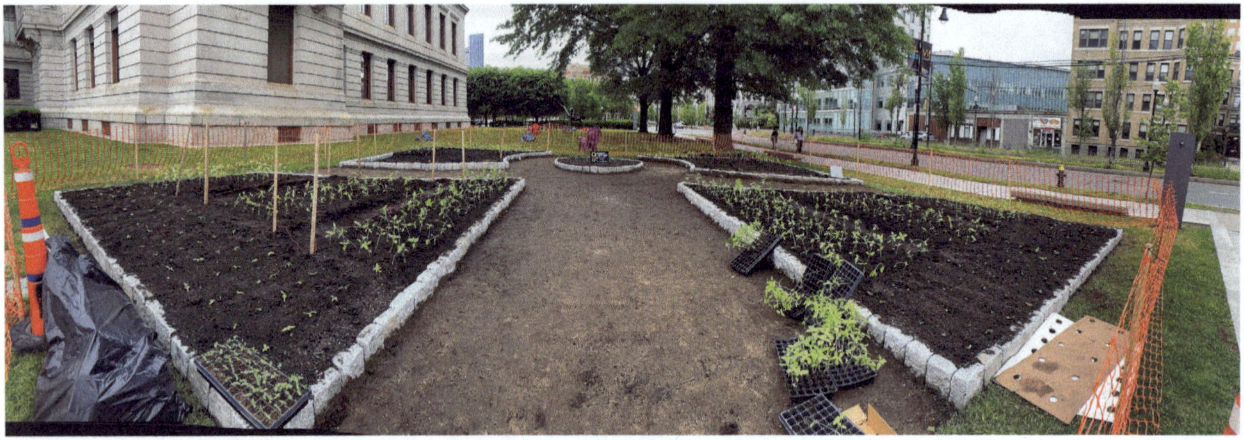

FIGURE 2.13 Ekua Holmes, *Radiant Community at the Museum of Fine Arts, Boston*, 2021. Roxbury Sunflower Project/Ekua Holmes

about that. It's about a Northeastern reflection of who we are as a people—and our connection to the lands and oceans here."[46]

With Holmes and James-Perry's projects, a single salient site on a Boston museum grounds becomes a nexus for multiple narratives to cacophonously converge through visual form. These may not be stories that were conceived in direct dialogue, but their physical proximities invite juxtaposition or simultaneous experience. Places, and their people, cannot be reduced to homogeneous or absolute stories, nor status quo primary versus counterviewing secondary perspectives. Cultural productions can both represent and manifest the vibrant, messy, contradictory, layered ecologies of local places. They can also form new directions for vital ways of being together in our shared places.

For example, Boston's Design Studio for Social Intervention (DS4SI) has spent years resisting the canons wrought through public design through an explicit methodology of interventionism. The studio defines intervention as "a gesture that is done by a set of people to bring attention to a social arrangement that may be adding to or a part of an ecology of a social problem."[47] For this innovative design studio, located in Upham's Corner, Boston, design solutions for social problems are artistic in nature. The studio values the impact and consequence of design within a symbolic sphere that Founder and Methodology and Strategy Director Kenneth Bailey describes as occurring "without the need for theory or explanation. When done right, the elegance of a gesture does the work." The kinds of interventions that DS4SI has produced for Boston include

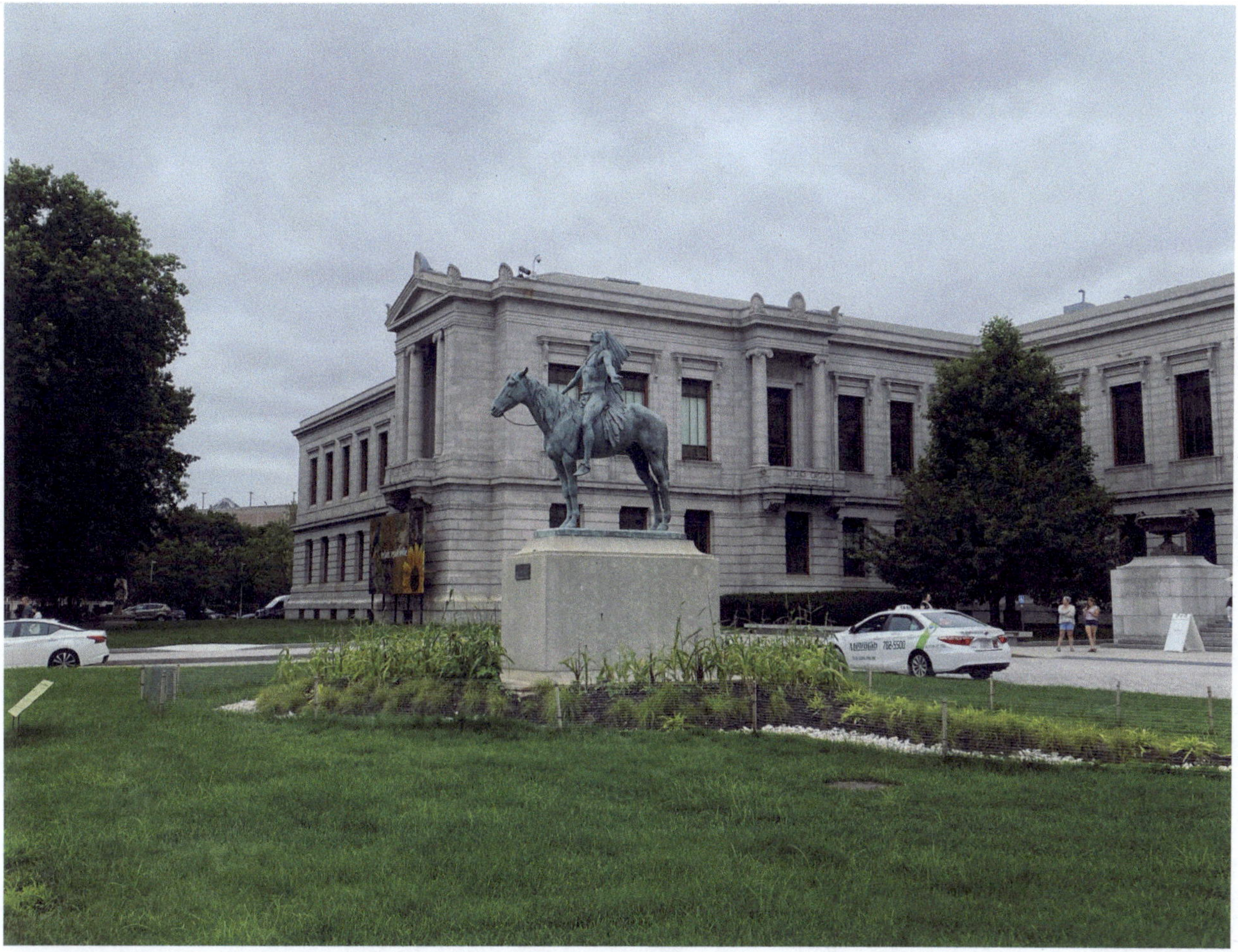

FIGURE 2.14 View of Elizabeth James-Perry's Horseshoe Crab Garden of Calais corn, beans, and sedge rimmed with quahog shell for *Raven Reshapes Boston: A Native Corn Garden at the MFA*, 2021

festivals, workshops, responsive labs, and centers for convening socially. These are discussed in one of three short video interviews produced for this book. Bailey notes that detouring away from canonical histories is not simply a recuperative maneuver of reclaiming or rewriting past narratives, but an active resistance to present operative systems, such as capitalism:

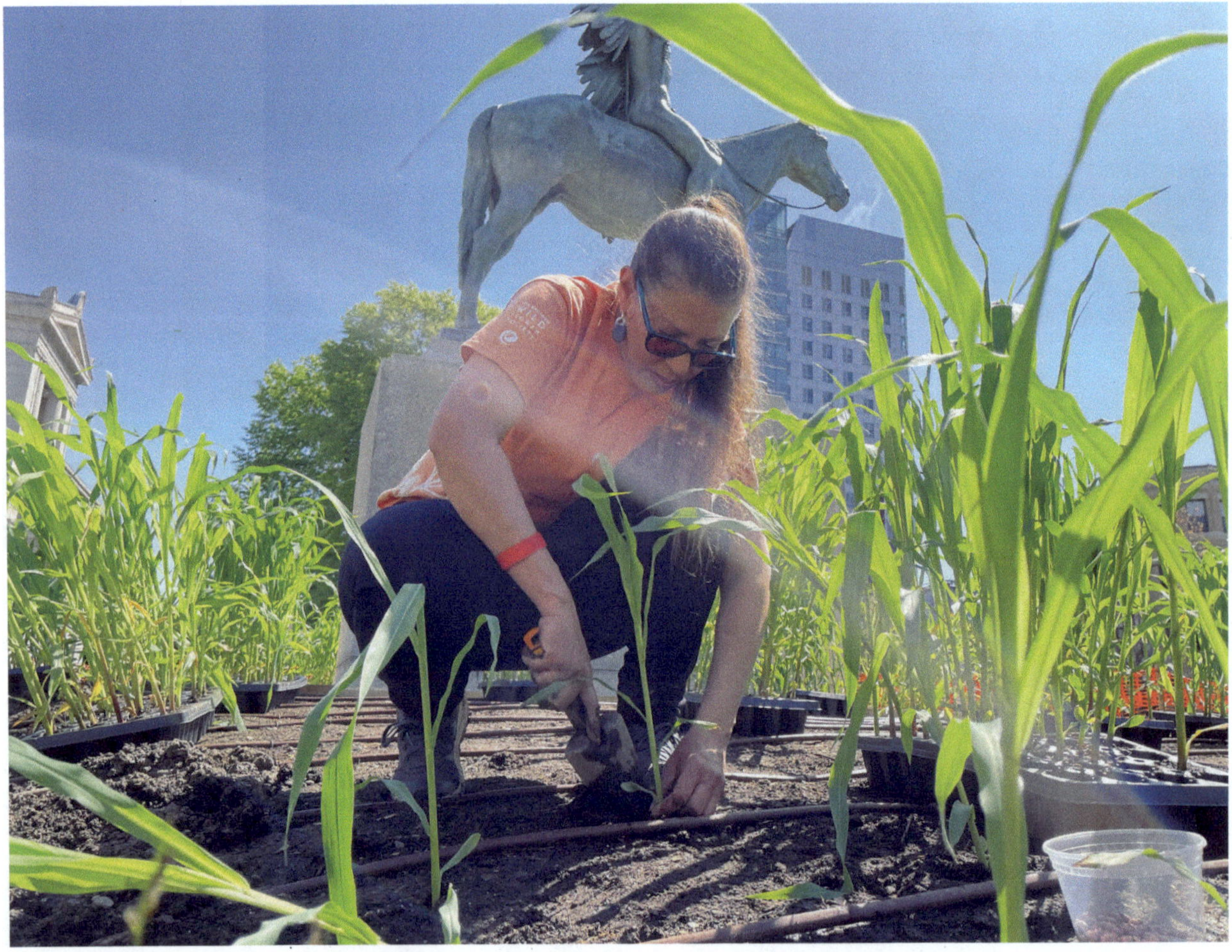

FIGURE 2.15 Artist Elizabeth James-Perry plants young corn for her Horseshoe Crab Garden as part of *Raven Reshapes Boston: A Native Corn Garden at the MFA*, 2021. Photo: Tess Lukey

Boston polices a little bit here and there and lets Whiteness do its work… You can use all the other buzzwords that continue to move things, like "safe," and "family-friendly," when in fact it's a moral and sense order that's being imposed on place and space. You have to decide how much do you want to fight that larger regime? … We are really interested in trying to unpack those things and continue to say Boston could be otherwise and could be a city where more people of color could actually be interested in being in the heart of the city, with the right sort of changes. Not necessarily just to participate in the heart of the city the way it is currently arranged as consumerist,

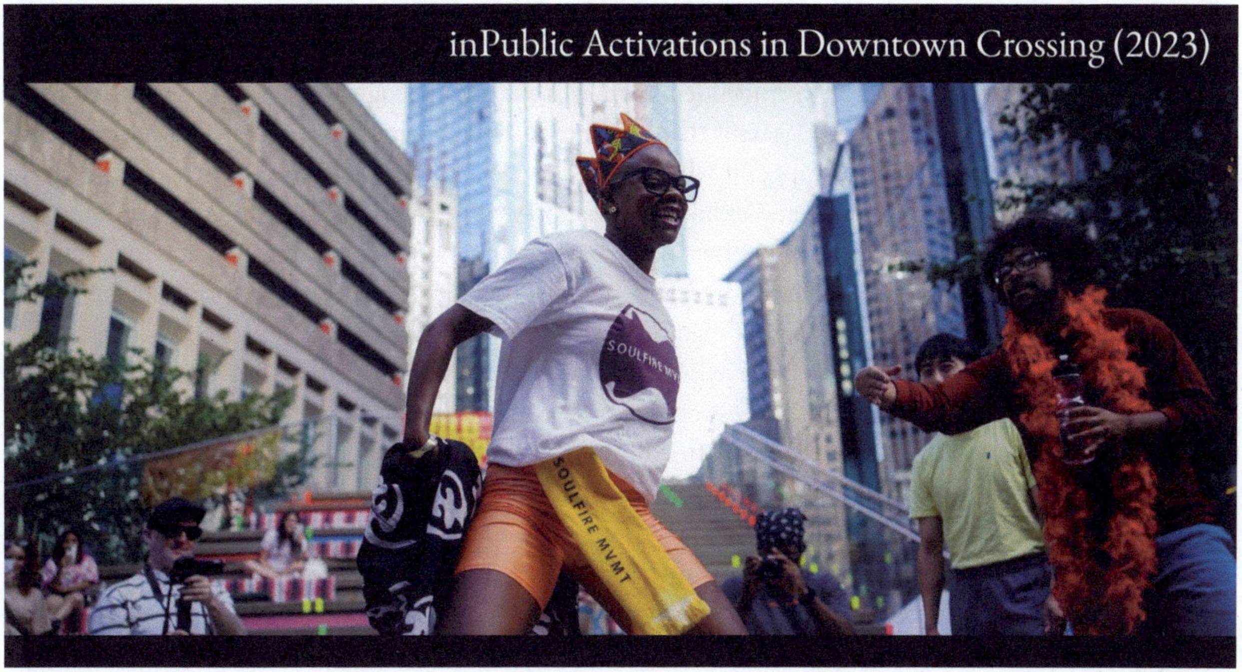

FIGURE 2.16 Still image from *Regime of the Sensible* roundtable video, produced for *Local Ecologies*, 2025. https://doi.org/10.3998/mpub.13189112.cmp.20

> but that the heart of the city could be rearranged such that other experiences don't necessarily have to be driven by consumption.[48]

Kenneth Bailey sat down for a video conversation with the editors of this volume on August 21, 2023. The video conversation covers sensory design, disinvestment, spatial justice, and the distribution of the sensible in Boston, MA. https://doi.org/10.3998/mpub.13189112.cmp.20

DIGGING IN

The landscape of New England is particularly rich with philosophical histories and patriotic mythologies that can obscure material truths—layered social and economic histories of place that include Indigenous land claims, the triangular trade, and military and industrial land use. The artists featured here bring the complex, even contradictory histories of the New England landscape into focus, revealing histories long occluded within conventional narratives, as well as the origins of contemporary injustices and environmental conditions. When we look at the use and narrativization of our local lands, especially as they are heralded as protected spaces rich with embedded memories, we must recognize that their stories are highly edited, most often through the power systems that lay claim to land ownership. Questions of what comprises a place, who determines its ownership, and what material effects come from those identifications can be asked anew through artistic practices and exhibitions that present opportunities for these explorations.

The remainder of this volume largely reflects on a particular set of artistic projects that comprised one exhibition, *Local Ecologies*, that is reconfigured here in an elaborated and intermedia form to create a new exhibitionary platform in print and digital mediums. In addition to directly revisiting and reconstituting in new form projects once presented in the exhibition, a series of roundtables convened over Zoom in high pandemic offer artist reflections on their experiences. Kenneth Bailey, co-founder of the aforementioned DS4SI, also offers an update. The changing nature of this exhibition series, including this book, reveals that the connotations of art and place are open-ended and relational in nature. The *Local Ecologies* project, introduced in the preceding chapter, includes artists who explore multiple striations of history in the common ground of local lands, and, through these histories, surface multiple forms of stake-claiming in the land. We recognize that these artistic projects will evolve in form and significance as our communities, collective memories, and shared values redefine places anew. An exhibition like *Local Ecologies* is never finished. This book inhabits a six-year span of time, between the early closing of *Local Ecologies* in March 2020 with the onset of the COVID pandemic and the point of this book's publication. It is a temporal marker that recognizes the everchanging nature of the places explored herein.

In the pages that follow, we explore how the artists and cultural collaborators who participated in the *Local Ecologies* project took very different methodological approaches, viewing explorations of the local as excavations of multiple histories and social facets simultaneously. In a roundtable discussion between participants in *Local Ecologies*, the artist María Magdelena Campos-Pons commented that:

> the nuances of how the materiality of one site starts to construct a physicality of being in another place—not just for people, but for the material itself—is something that has been fundamental for my research and investigation, because it created for me a much more nuanced and subliminal presentation of how we define geography, how we define territory, and how we design the authenticity of the ground that we are standing on.[49]

This is not, and never has been, neutral ground. We are responsible for how we delineate, cultivate, narrativize, and provide or restrict access to the places that are our commons.

An example of reflective, multivocal narrativizing of place is artist Sarah Kanouse and historian Nicholas Brown's collaborative tours of Boston Harbor with Faries Gray, Sagamore (chief) of the Massachusett Tribe at Ponkapoag. These tours, hosted by UMass Boston, redefine ideas of territory. They present Boston Harbor as an ongoing, everchanging space through annual journeys through the waters and ground of the Deer Island. These journeys are collective explorations that rethink the meaning of these spaces collaboratively and as a community. Gray also conducts tours of Boston Harbor for the National Park Service that counter common settler-colonial assumptions of Indigenous absence from this landscape. These tours impart a fundamental message: "When the first Europeans arrived in the late 16th century, bringing with them disease, war, and a hunger for more and more land, millions of indigenous people were killed, and more were displaced to the point that many believe there are no indigenous people left in the Boston area…Nothing could be farther from the truth."[50]

The artistic methodologies explored in this volume are based on research into "local" conditions, behaviors, and materials, *and* how such locally designated propositions are complicated by the diverse realpolitik of the local as it actually is—occupied and in many ways encumbered by many persons, organisms, and histories. Moreover, the premises of "local ecologies" explored in this volume are necessarily entangled in networks outside of any specific locally defined boundaries, such as, in the case of Campos-Pons's research, the complexities of sugar exchange within the global system of Black Atlantic modernity. In this sense, we can explore how being "on the ground" never only means being in one place. Through these investigations we see how one place contains multitudes, and how being in place means seeing the many places that render one site through its systems, ecologies, and cultural histories. Places are never neutral, they are heavy, deep, complex, and ongoing. This book attempts to honor that condition by inviting multiple, and often unfinished, takes on the places that make up Eastern Massachusetts.

Part II

Local Ecologies

CHAPTER 3

Introduction: *Local Ecologies*

This volume convenes interdisciplinary artists, scholars, and activists to explore the layered histories and diverse ecosystems of Eastern Massachusetts, from the harbors of Boston and New Bedford to the canals of the Merrimack River.[1] The volume is inspired by the artists Dan Borelli, María Magdalena Campos-Pons, Duy Hoàng, Sarah Kanouse and Nicholas Brown, Plotform (Jane Marsching and Andi Sutton), Evelyn Rydz, and Andrew Yang, who participated in *Local Ecologies*, a series of research-based art projects and public programs developed with UMass Boston, Dartmouth, and Lowell between 2018 and 2020. The initiative is chronicled here along with critical reflections on the role of regionalism in the global present, and art as opportunity for transdisciplinary explorations among historians, scientists, activists, and cultural producers. The initiative included a dynamic exhibition that changed and developed responsively in each of its three venues, forming the headquarters for a larger creative research initiative that extended beyond the gallery walls. It encompassed artist-led walking tours, boat trips, poetry workshops, summits on vision and contamination, new research directions, and other programmatic endeavors. These investigations commingle histories of indigeneity, immigration, "nature," science, and other disciplines. This volume collects the diverse artworks, scholarly essays, interviews, video, and other documents produced for that initiative.

Eastern Massachusetts is hard to see. Even as Indigenous and colonial place names are inscribed on the landscape, histories are obscured. In the everyday passages of our commutes and errands we notice how the transcendentalist cult of nature, associated with landscapes like Walden Pond, converges with the military-industrial complex along the Route 128 technology corridor—home to Raytheon, Boston Dynamics, and many other developers of military technologies—through the suburban landscapes of Lexington, Concord, and Lincoln. "Nature," in the transcendentalist sense, has a complicated cultural and scientific history in Eastern Massachusetts: Rachel Carson was moved to write her famous tract *Silent Spring* after receiving a letter in 1958 from Duxbury resident Olga Owens Huckins, an amateur ornithologist who discovered dead songbirds throughout her property after the state sprayed DDT to control the mosquito population. The notion of toxins in our air and water invisible to the eye was a prominent anxiety of the nuclear age. The theme of visibilities informs the *Local Ecologies* initiative, but so too does the concept of latent and invisible memories, ideas, dangers, and hopes that remain embedded in our landscapes. So much goes unseen—or unsaid—yet shapes our social and economic interactions or affects our bodies.

In fall 2017, John D. Kelly published a speculative essay in *Anthropological Quarterly* with the title "New Bedford, Capital of the 19th Century?"[2] Drawing from Walter Benjamin's essays that evolved into *The Arcades Project*, Kelly's essay considers how interpretive framing shapes history: why not identify New Bedford, the "city that lit the world" (through the oil extraction of the whaling industry), as the center of a developing modernity, a key counterpart to Paris, City of Light?[3] The essay particularly looks at the figure of abolitionist and anti-slavery orator Frederick Douglass, who made his home in New Bedford in the late 1830s. Kelly considers the ways the contemporary tourism industry and agents of historical preservation in New Bedford revivify memories of Douglass, the historical whaling industry, and Herman Melville (whose Ishmael overnights and prays in the town of New Bedford prior to heading out to sea from Nantucket in the ill-fated *Pequod*; Melville's own whaling expedition launched from New Bedford in early 1841). A particularly beloved object of historical and cultural interpretation in the New Bedford landscape, also discussed by Kelly in his essay, is a pulpit shaped like a whaling ship in the historic Seamen's Bethel. This pulpit was retrofitted to appear this way in 1961, after a 1956 film version of *Moby Dick* included a pulpit in this shape, and tourists visiting New Bedford were disappointed not to encounter it in the historic site. In other words, a historical landmark was adapted to look more like the film version, in order to better suit the expectations of contemporary visitors. In this way, an artistic tweak to a physical environment linked historical imagination to the visibilities of actual historical sites.

The forms comprising our natural and built environments are quite literally shaped by cultural interpretation. Arbiters of interpretation, preservation, and protection of New Bedford, such as the New Bedford Whaling National Historical Park, the New Bedford Historical Society, and the Whaling Museum (along with many other cultural partners), recognize and commemorate histories of the local textile industry, whaling culture, abolitionist activism, and more recent histories of toxic PCBs in the New Bedford Harbor through statuary, murals, read-a-thons, and interpretive signage. During the course of *Local Ecologies*, participating artists also engaged regional histories using a great range of interpretive means. These artworks became inroads to understanding matters of local environmental and social concern.

One *Local Ecologies* commission, *Dear Harbor Radio*, was a participatory project by a two-woman collective called Plotform. In the summer and fall of 2019, the artists—Jane D. Marsching and Andi

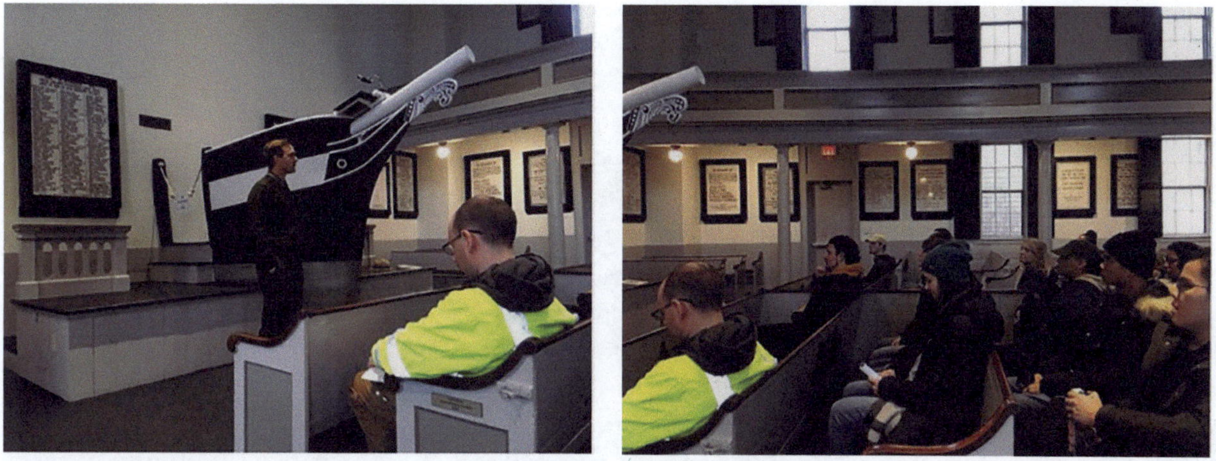

FIGURE 3.1 Ranger Andrew Schnetzer tours students in Rebecca Uchill's "Processing Place" class through the Seamen's Bethel, with ship-shaped pulpit in the background. February 11, 2020. Photos: Rebecca Uchill

Sutton—toured the New Bedford region, pulling a mobile writing/recording/radio station by bicycle and boat. During workshops and encounters at UMass Dartmouth, the Whaling Museum, the New Bedford Whaling National Historical Park, and other venues, the artists invited participants to collectively reflect on the climate crisis and current ecological emergencies through a lens of love and cross-species empathy, prompting passersby to write love letters to nonhuman species. The ensuing recordings, which include letters read aloud, music from the New Bedford Sea Shanty Chorus, and sounds of whales, bees, and the environments of Buzzards Bay, were continually broadcast on a shortwave radio frequency from their bike-mounted workstation while on the move and while parked in the galleries. During the *Local Ecologies* exhibition, College of Visual and Performing Arts undergraduate student and arts ambassador Gina Pantalone ran two public letter-writing workshops. The artists' SoundCloud associated with the project is an ongoing, perpetually developing archive of these encounters that allowed us to better see—and hear—a record of the changing landscape in New Bedford, through the tributes of its human constituents to their nonhuman cohabitants.

A 2010 article by Caroline A. Jones and Peter Galison articulates problems of visibility differently. They write about the "production of invisibility" in response to the Deepwater Horizon oil spill in the Gulf of Mexico, the "system of images and occlusions, or seeing and unseeing, that marks the response to ecological disaster" in the media.[4] How do we unsee given forms of cultural interpretation, in order to see

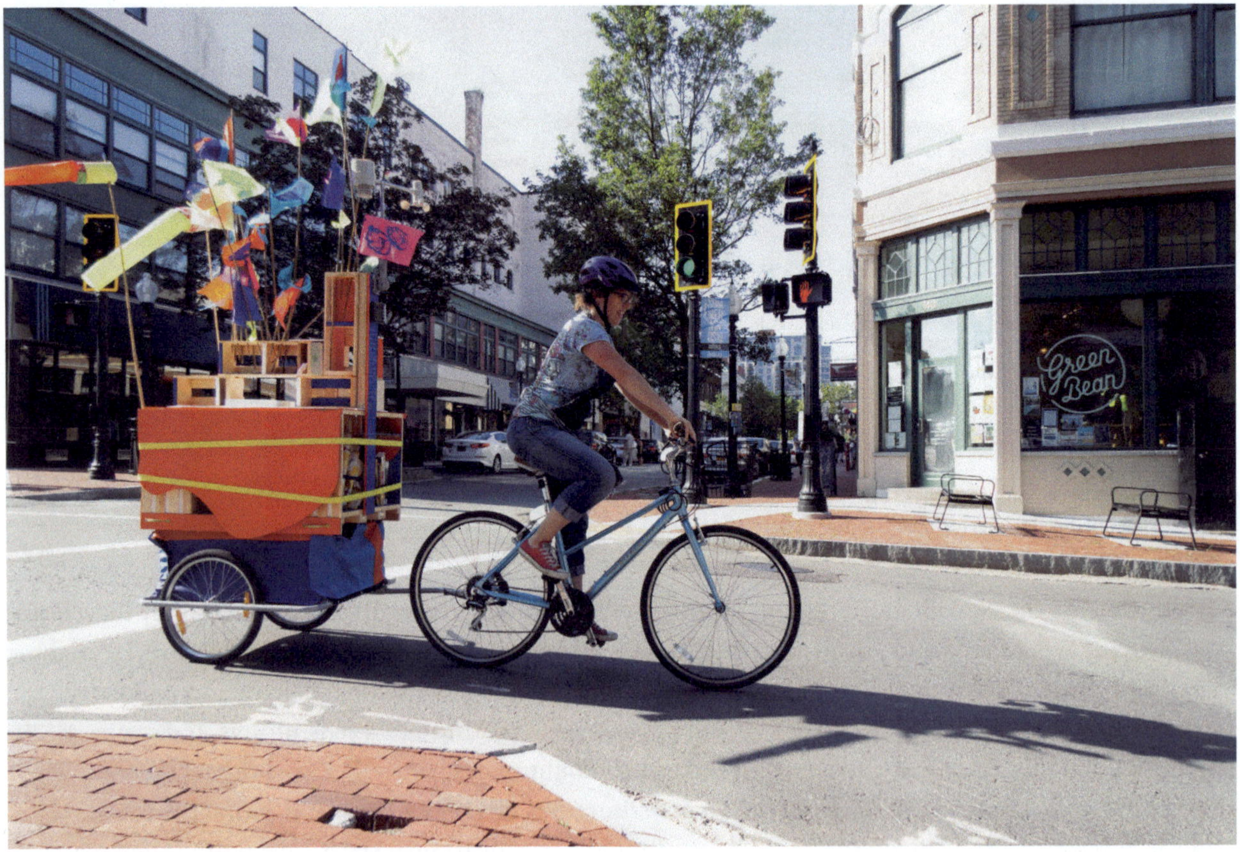

FIGURE 3.2 Plotform, *Dear Harbor Radio*, 2019. Photo: Viera Levitt

expanded landscapes that may have been occluded from view? Artists can produce new modes of perceiving and experiencing the landscapes we inhabit, alongside new historical frameworks for interpreting place that reject/defy/move past entrenched canonical histories, giving material form to the systems—ecological, infrastructural, economic, institutional—that define a place. The pages that follow offer new modalities for interpreting place and landscape in the contemporary moment.

CHAPTER 4
Ecologies of Acknowledgment

In this chapter, artists Sarah Kanouse and Nick Brown, along with UMass Boston curator Sam Toabe, reflect on *Ecologies of Acknowledgment*, a video artwork catalyzed by collaborative archival and immersive research into the Indigenous history and present use of Deer Island in Boston Harbor—a site of imprisonment for Native peoples in the seventeenth century, and current home to a wastewater treatment facility. This ongoing series of engagements—some of which involve purposefully anonymous contributors—is hard to encapsulate in brief. In one program offered in alliance with this project, Elizabeth Solomon (Massachusett), Nia Holley (Nipmuc), and Faries Gray (Massachusett) offered boat tours of this island. The island is a place of insufficient memorial, and vital tribute, which reveals the act of memorializing to be an active and ongoing gesture. Stories of dispossession, colonialization, and migration are not matters of the past. How do these stories continue to pervade the fabric of our lives, and how does their embodied or materialized retelling resist the obdurate nature of preservation and monumentality?

ECOLOGIES OF ACKNOWLEDGMENT AND *INDIGENOUS BOSTON HARBOR*

Sam Toabe

Sarah Kanouse and Nicholas Brown's *Ecologies of Acknowledgment* and the companion *Indigenous Boston Harbor* boat tour were commissioned by the University Hall Gallery as part of *Local Ecologies*. Each project focuses on the complicated land-use histories of Deer Island in Boston Harbor. During Metacomet's Rebellion (also known as King Philip's War), Deer Island was the site of an internment camp where hundreds of Native peoples, who had been forced off their lands, were incarcerated by colonists during the winter of 1675–76. Nearly half died there, having been stranded without adequate food or shelter during the harsh winter months. An interpretive sign near the main parking lot for the Deer Island Public Access Area explains, "Since colonial days, Deer Island has served as a detention center for American Indians, a quarantine station and hospital for immigrants, an asylum for the city's social outcasts and the poor, a reformatory for juvenile delinquents, an orphanage, a prison for petty criminals, and a military post." Deer Island is now home to Boston's wastewater treatment plant, which has transformed Boston Harbor from one of the nation's most polluted, contaminated for centuries with waste and raw sewage, to one of the country's cleanest over the past thirty years.

In Kanouse and Brown's video installation, *Ecologies of Acknowledgment*, the plant "functions as a crucible for ecopolitical relationships," connecting the island's complicated past, present, and future.[1] Through archival research at the Healey Library at UMass Boston and the Massachusetts State Archives, site visits, and interviews with several members of local Indigenous tribes (Massachusett, Nipmuc, and Natick Nipmuc), the artists developed a video installation that tells a more complete history of Deer Island told through oral histories of the Harbor Islands and commentary on contemporary climate justice from Indigenous perspectives. The installation, as presented at the UMass Boston, included a stack of loose leaf, letterpress prints for viewers to take with them. Developed in collaboration with Elizabeth Solomon, a member of the Massachusett Tribe at Ponkapoag, the prints served as a subversive land acknowledgment. They allowed the artwork to extend beyond the confines of the gallery and our campus. Traversing public and private spaces, it challenged common conceptions of the efficacy of land acknowledgments that often begin and end with listing whose territory we reside on during public events. When the exhibition traveled from Boston to Dartmouth and Lowell, the artists presented a larger, limited edition, color version of the takeaway print that was annotated by the artists and gallery staff by hand to reflect the territories of different tribes' unceded lands occupied by the campuses. As the artists explain, "*Ecologies of Acknowledgment* is an attempt to create a land acknowledgment that does more than recognize Native territory, asking instead what it means to accept the relationships and responsibilities that come with living on occupied land."[2]

Alongside *Ecologies of Acknowledgment*, Kanouse and Brown developed a now ongoing eco-political education public program in collaboration with and led by local Indigenous leaders entitled *Indigenous Boston Harbor*, a boat tour that further explores the Indigenous histories of Deer Island and the Boston Harbor Islands. Produced as part of UMass Boston's public art program, Arts on the Point, the group exploration is composed of a guided boat tour that launches from UMass Boston's Fox Point aboard the university's marine vessel, the *Columbia Point*. Over its past three iterations, the tour has charted a course through the harbor where sites along the route to Deer Island echo and expand upon the histories shared in *Ecologies of Acknowledgment*, framed by a critical telling of the Indigenous histories and contemporary land uses of the unceded waterways and islands. Each year, the boat has landed on Deer Island where the participants disembark for a walking tour of the site where the atrocious history of the internment camp took place. For the participants, leaving our campus to travel on the water, to be on site, and venture into the land that these histories are linked to has been powerful and expansive. Each of the three tours have consisted of over 80 participants, including students, professors, park rangers, scientists, historians, and members of the Indigenous communities of Eastern Massachusetts. We have all experienced something more vivid than the facts and figures can convey about this seemingly distant past. By bringing us to the locations where these difficult histories took place and continue to resonate, the Indigenous historians and artists have framed our current moment in context with the past, implicating our choices in acknowledging or marginalizing these violent histories.

The project's first run in the fall of 2019 was led by historians and activists Elizabeth Solomon (Massachusett at Ponkapoag), Nia Holley (Nipmuc), and Faries Gray (Massachusett at Ponkapoag). Both Solomon and Holley were contributors to Kanouse and Brown's research in the development of *Ecologies of Acknowledgment*. This iteration focused on the political histories of the islands and the lack of significant memorials or proper signage in the public park on Deer Island, managed by the Boston Department of Conservation and Recreation, commemorating the history of the island. They have also touched upon other contemporary responses to these histories such as the annual twenty-mile Sacred Paddle down the Charles River to Deer Island that members of the Wampanoag and Nipmuc tribes undertake each October to memorialize the island's tragic history. *Indigenous Boston Harbor* has since grown in support and attendance, with Solomon and Gray continuing to guide two tours in 2022. These tours touched upon the histories and complicated contemporary land management cases of other islands and waterways in the Boston Harbor, such as the recent, controversial demolition of the bridge to the Long Island substance use recovery center and the archaeological digs taking place on Moon Island, developments for which Gray was consulted. In October of 2024, we produced our sixth and seventh tours of *Indigenous Boston Harbor* with Elizabeth Solomon and Faries Gray. Moving forward, we plan to host two tours annually, maintaining and strengthening Arts on the Point's commitment to the project.

EXTENDED ECOLOGIES OF ACKNOWLEDGMENT

Nicholas Brown and Sarah Kanouse

These are *Indigenous* waters and lands. These are *Massachusett* waters and lands.

Boston Harbor contains thirty-four islands, ranging in size from less than 1 acre to 274 acres. The film *Ecologies of Acknowledgment* addressed the painful history of one of them: Deer Island, site of both Boston's groundbreaking wastewater treatment center and the location of the first prison camp for Indigenous people in what would become the United States. The two ongoing projects offered here extend the central argument of the film: that acknowledgment of the land's Indigenous histories requires a fundamental rethinking of the infrastructures of the present and a commitment to be in better relationship with the Native people for whom these lands and waters were named.

Kanouse and Brown's video essay, *Ecologies of Acknowledgment,* 2019, addressed histories of Deer Island's occupation, human use, and the politics of naming: https://doi.org/10.3998/mpub.13189112.cmp.24

Indigenous Boston Harbor is a half-day boat tour of Boston Harbor and the Harbor Islands and a walking tour of Deer Island. The tour highlights past, present, and future Indigenous relationships—*especially Massachusett relationships*—with the harbor and the islands, particularly Deer, Thompson, Peddocks, Long, and Moon Islands. The tour also emphasizes Massachusett relationships with the Neponset River, which empties into the harbor at Dorchester Bay. The free tour enables community members to get out on the water, walk on the islands, and listen to Indigenous leaders. It also allows tribal members to visit special places and share stories among themselves, including intergenerational and intertribal sharing.

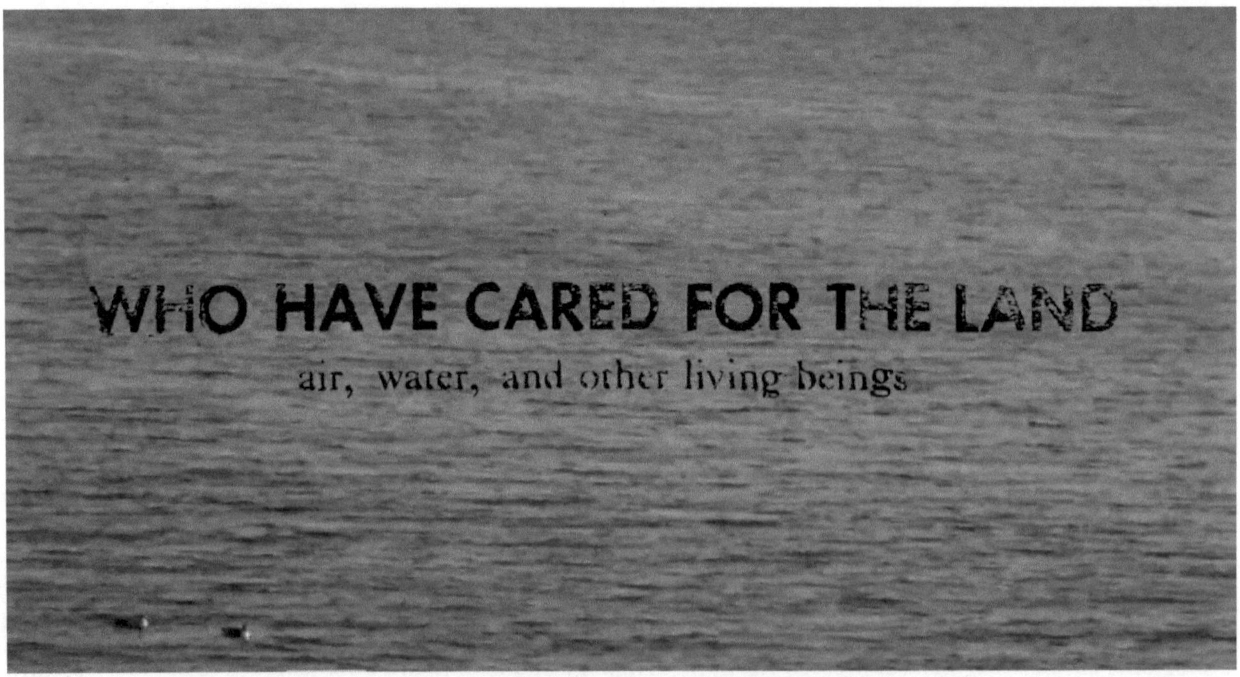

FIGURE 4.1 Still from Sarah Kanouse and Nicholas Brown, *Ecologies of Acknowledgment,* 2019

The first tour took place on October 8, 2019, as part of the *Local Ecologies* exhibition at UMass Boston. It was led by Elizabeth Solomon, a member of the Massachusett Tribe at Ponkapoag, Nia Holley, a member of the Nipmuc Nation, and Faries Gray, Sagamore of the Massachusett Tribe at Ponkapaog. After a three-year hiatus due to the pandemic, the tours resumed in 2022. Elizabeth Solomon and Faries Gray led tours on October 18 and 22. Together, we are committed to running the tours annually.

Every tour is different, in terms of the itinerary, the speakers, the weather, and the stories that are shared. To date, the tours have all included a visit to Deer Island, which is dominated by the Deer Island Wastewater Treatment Plant, the second largest sewage treatment plant in the United States. Deer Island is one of thirty-four islands that comprise Boston Harbor Islands, a national park area that was established in 1996.

Centering Massachusett perspectives, the tour considers how Deer Island's "varied past" is interpreted by the National Park Service and the ten other agencies that make up the Boston Harbor Islands Partnership. A sign on the island briefly outlines this varied and contested past: "Since colonial days, Deer Island has served as a detention center for American Indians, a quarantine station and hospital for immigrants, an asylum for the city's social outcasts and the poor, a reformatory for juvenile delinquents, an orphanage, a prison for petty criminals, and a military post." How does this varied past—which conspicuously begins in the colonial period—inform the present and future of Deer Island and the other Harbor Islands? How do these narratives—colonial narratives—influence the ways these islands are managed and used today? And how might they be used and managed differently? In our present moment of rising seas and climate breakdown, how do we understand the role of colonization as one of the drivers of these changes?

During the 364 days per year when the *Indigenous Boston Harbor* tour does not take place, *Deer Island: a counter-tour* offers a more individual opportunity to consider these questions. The single-sheet zine, available here as a free download, complicates the narrative presented at marked sites on the Deer Island walking path. Originally developed for Caroline Jones's *Landscape Experience* class at MIT when *Indigenous Boston Harbor* tours were paused during the COVID-19 pandemic, the zine pairs quotations—whether from existing signage, historians, philosophers, or the *Ecologies of Acknowledgment* film itself—with questions that can be productively posed at the established vista points on the official tour. These include questions about whose memory landscapes are represented on the island and how, the temporality involved in the view of Boston from Deer Island, and the stakes of considering the island primarily as triumph of green engineering at a moment of escalating climate change directly traceable to the eco-techno-political disruptions of colonization.

Kanouse and Brown created a downloadable and printable zine that provides a self-guided tour of Deer Island and its Indigenous and settler-colonial histories (https://doi.org/10.3998/mpub.13189112.cmp.25). Instructions for assembly are available at https://doi.org/10.3998/mpub.13189112.cmp.26

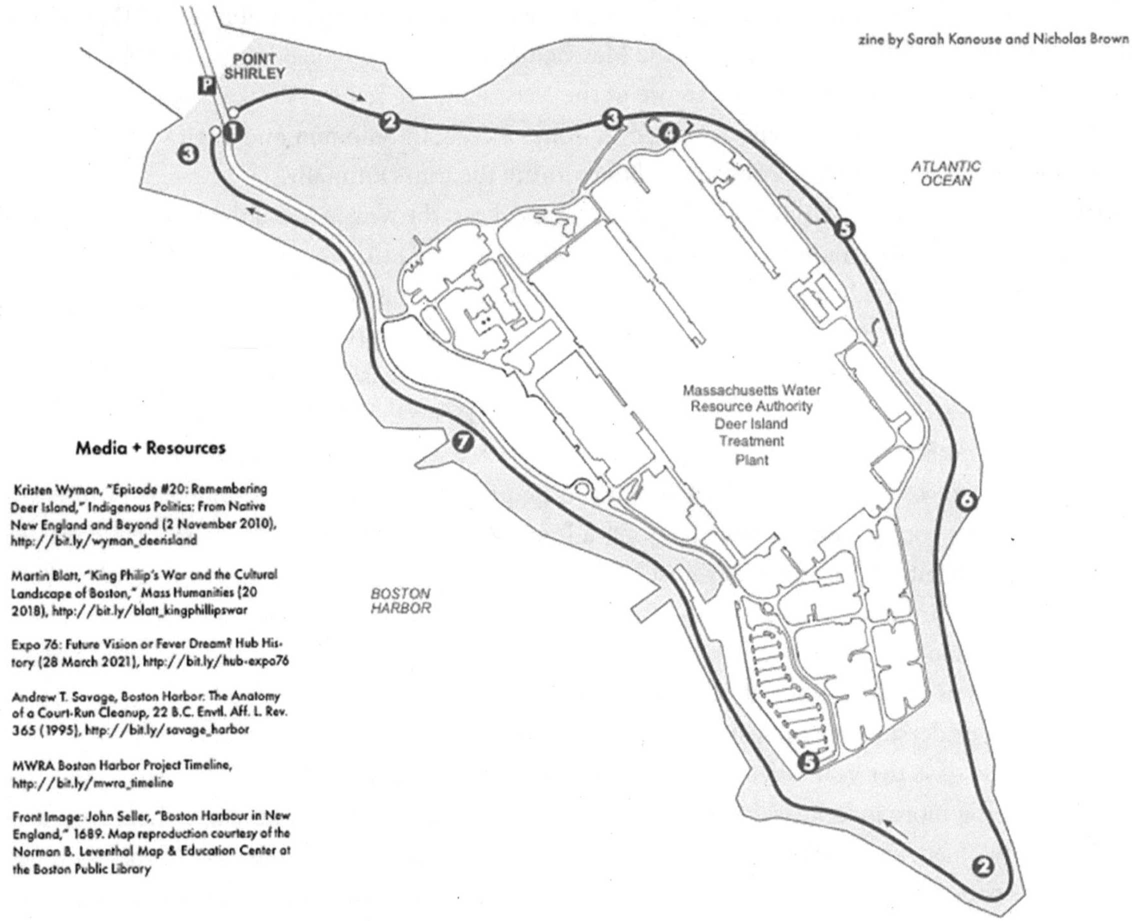

FIGURE 4.2 Page from Sarah Kanouse and Nicholas Brown, *Deer Island Counter-Tour Zine*, 2019

Both *Indigenous Boston Harbor* and *Deer Island: a counter-tour* provide opportunities to reflect the present-day legacies of settler colonialism more generally. Highlighting relationships with the land and water that have endured and evolved despite centuries of violence and dispossession, the tour shows how Boston Harbor and the Harbor Islands remain Indigenous space. Like the broader *Ecologies of Acknowledgment* project, the tour and zine offer an opportunity to reflect on the practice and politics of land acknowledgments, which are necessary but insufficient gestures of accountability to Indigenous peoples in the colonial present. For non-Indigenous participants, they are invitations to re-orient oneself within Indigenous space, to reimagine relationships with Indigenous peoples, and to continue the long and difficult process of reckoning and repair.

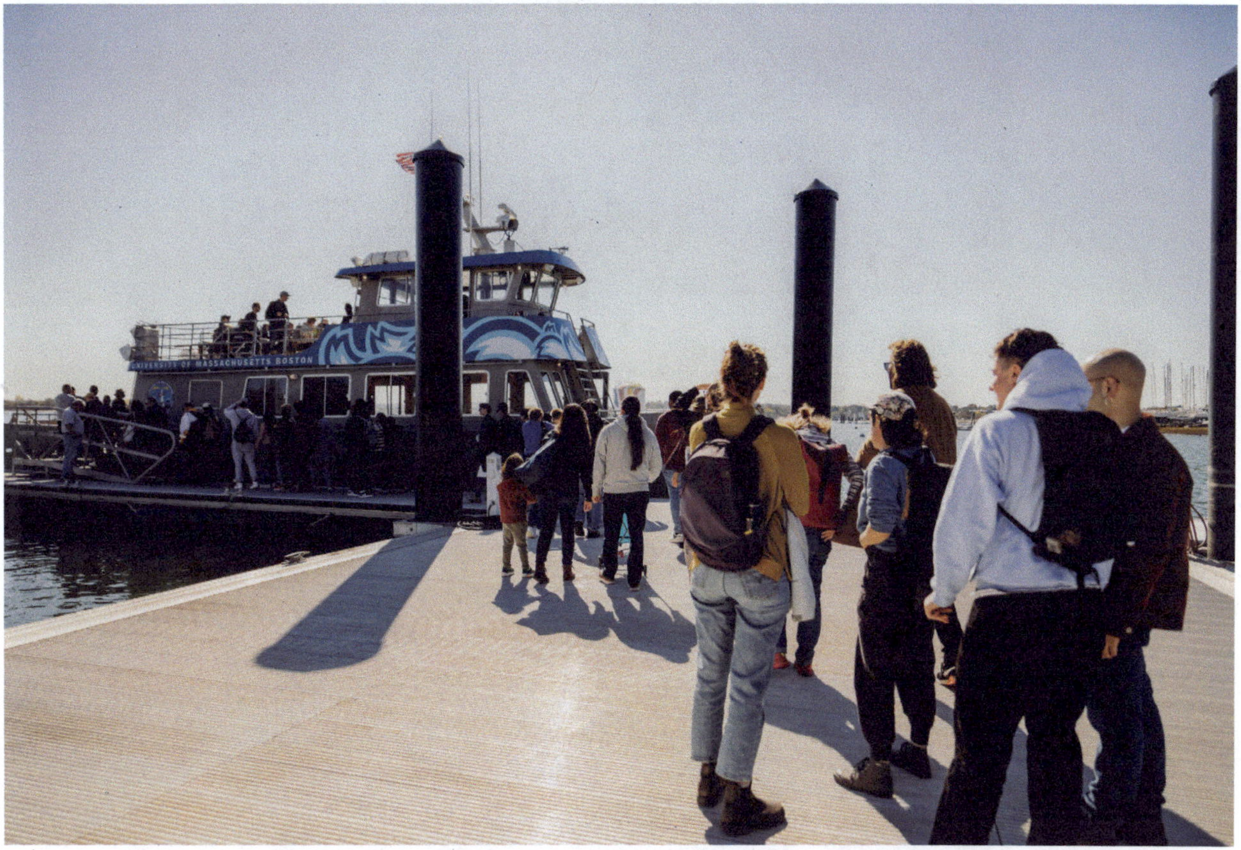

FIGURE 4.3 Participants in Indigenous Boston Harbor board the boat at the University of Massachusetts Boston dock on October 22, 2022. Photograph by Mel Taing

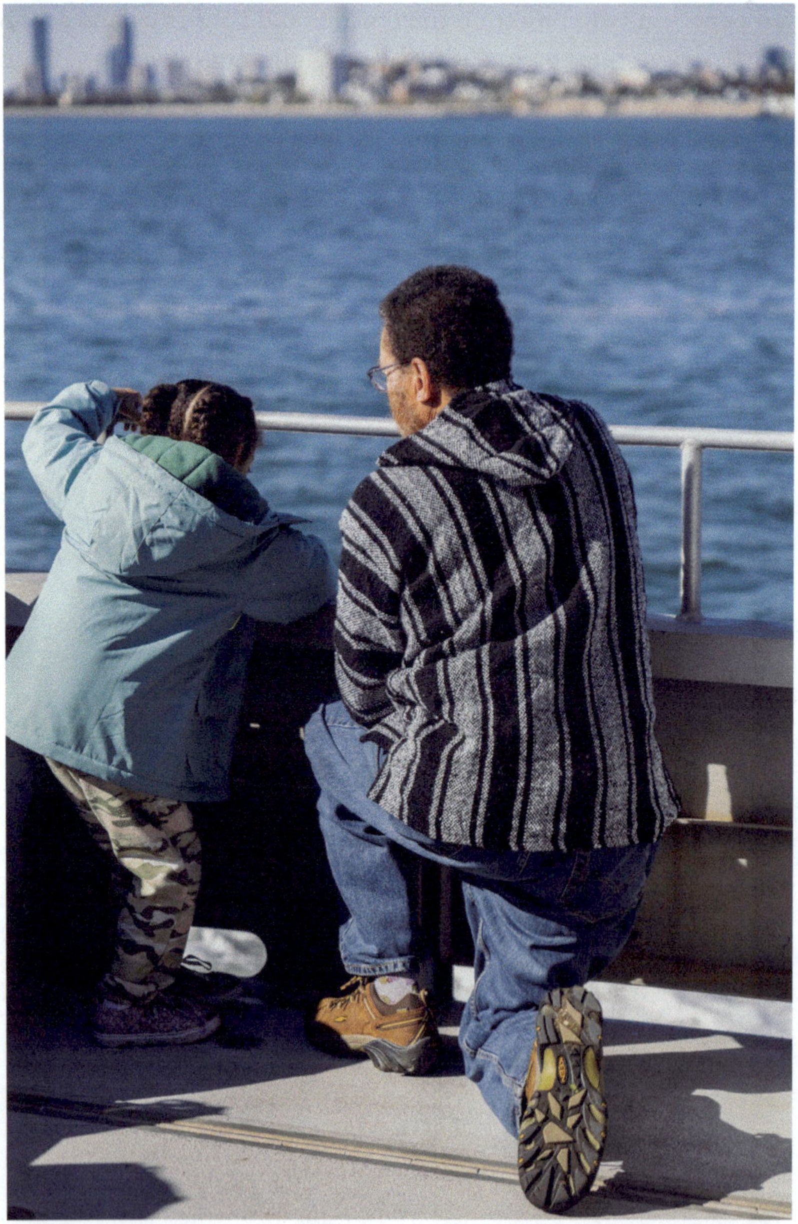

FIGURE 4.4 Informal childcare on the Indigenous Boston Harbor boat tour, October 22, 2022. Photograph by Mel Taing

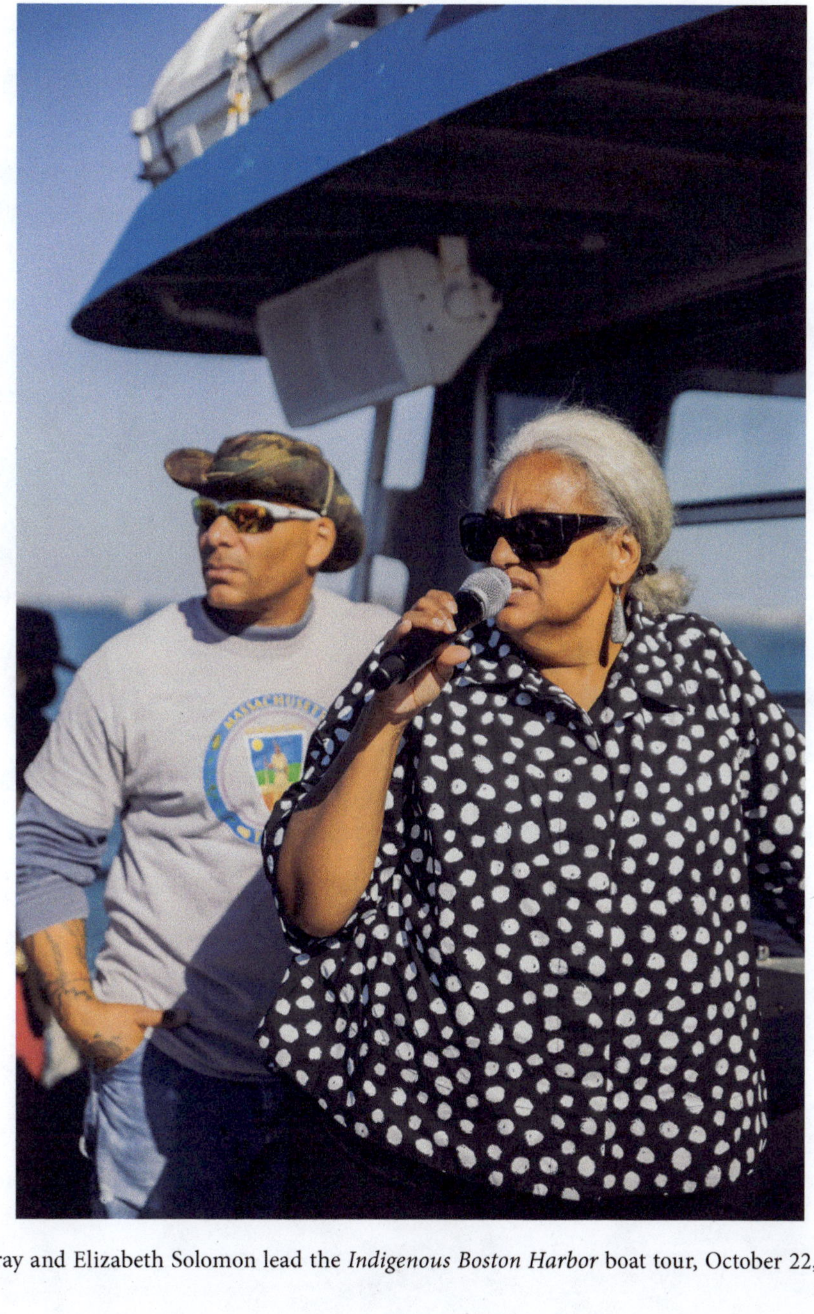

FIGURE 4.5 Faries Gray and Elizabeth Solomon lead the *Indigenous Boston Harbor* boat tour, October 22, 2022. Photograph by Mel Taing

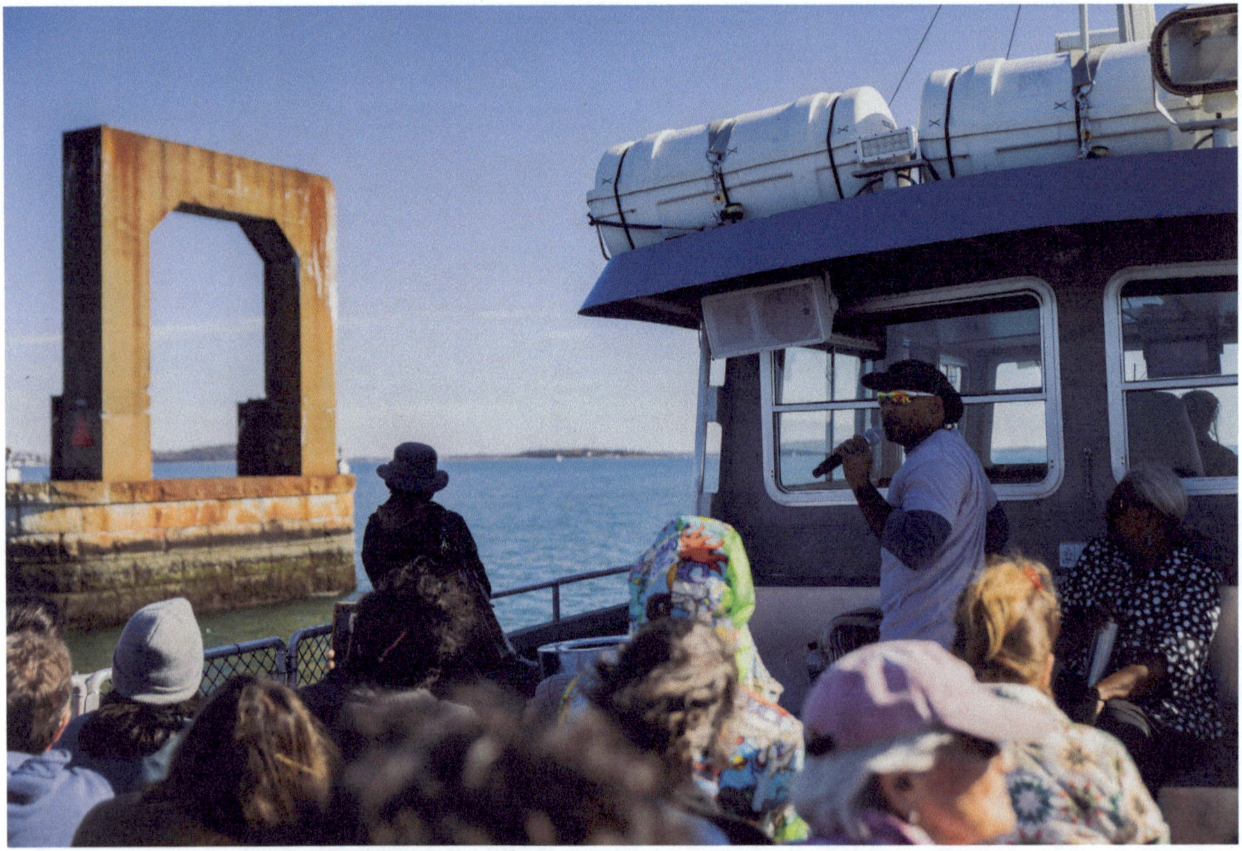

FIGURE 4.6 Faries Gray speaks about Long Island as the tour passes the footings of the demolished Long Island Bridge, October 22, 2022. Photograph by Mel Taing

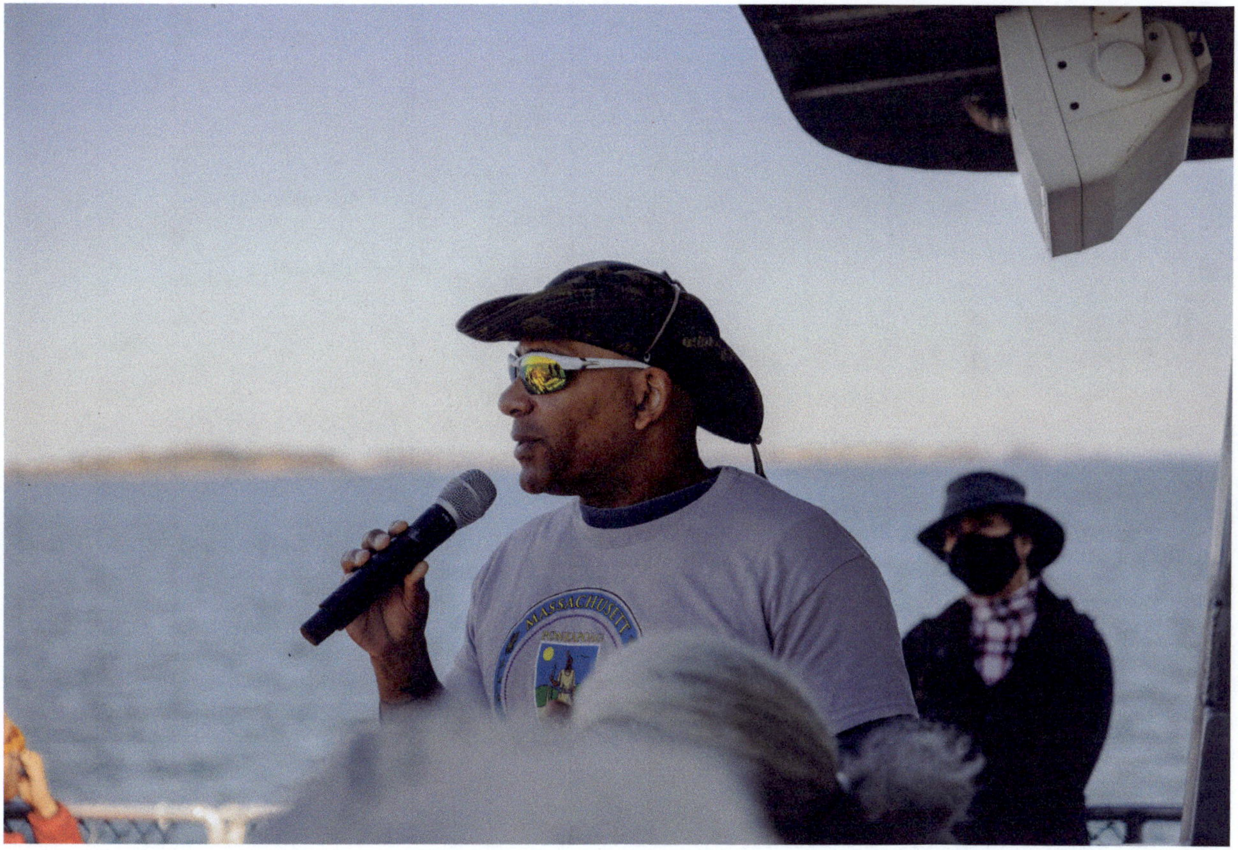

FIGURE 4.7 Faries Gray on the *Indigenous Boston Harbor* tour, October 22, 2022. Photograph by Mel Taing

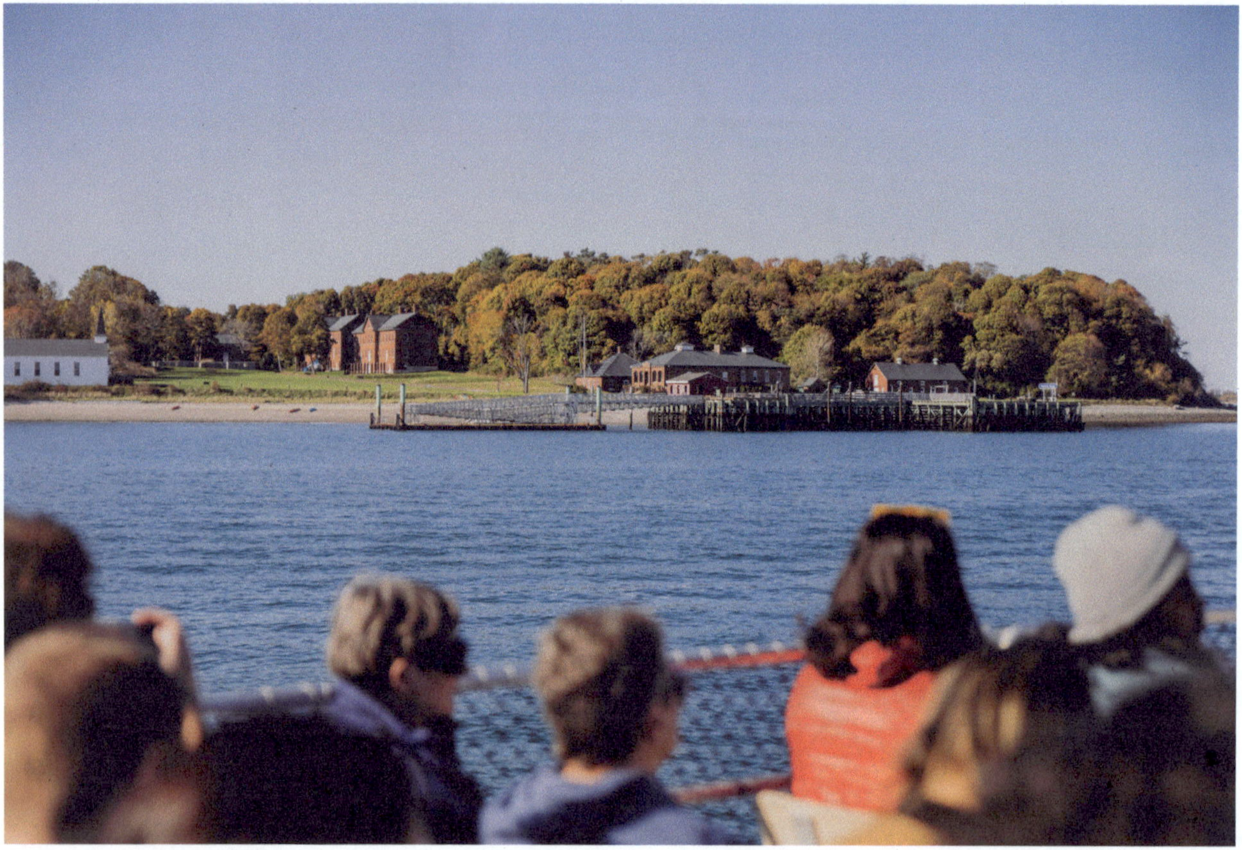

FIGURE 4.8 *Indigenous Boston Harbor* boat tour passes by the dock on Peddocks Island, October 22, 2022. Photograph by Mel Taing

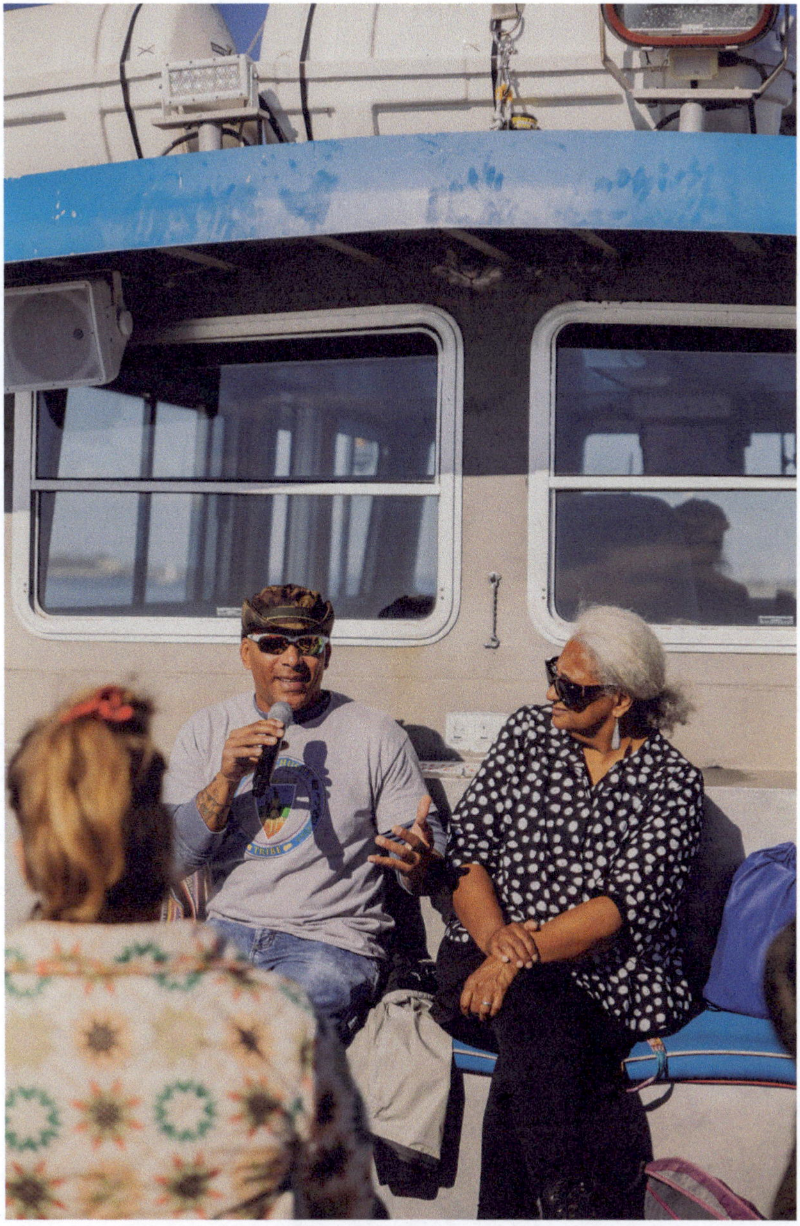

FIGURE 4.9 Faries Gray and Elizabeth Solomon in dialogue on the *Indigenous Boston Harbor* boat tour, October 22, 2022. Photograph by Mel Taing

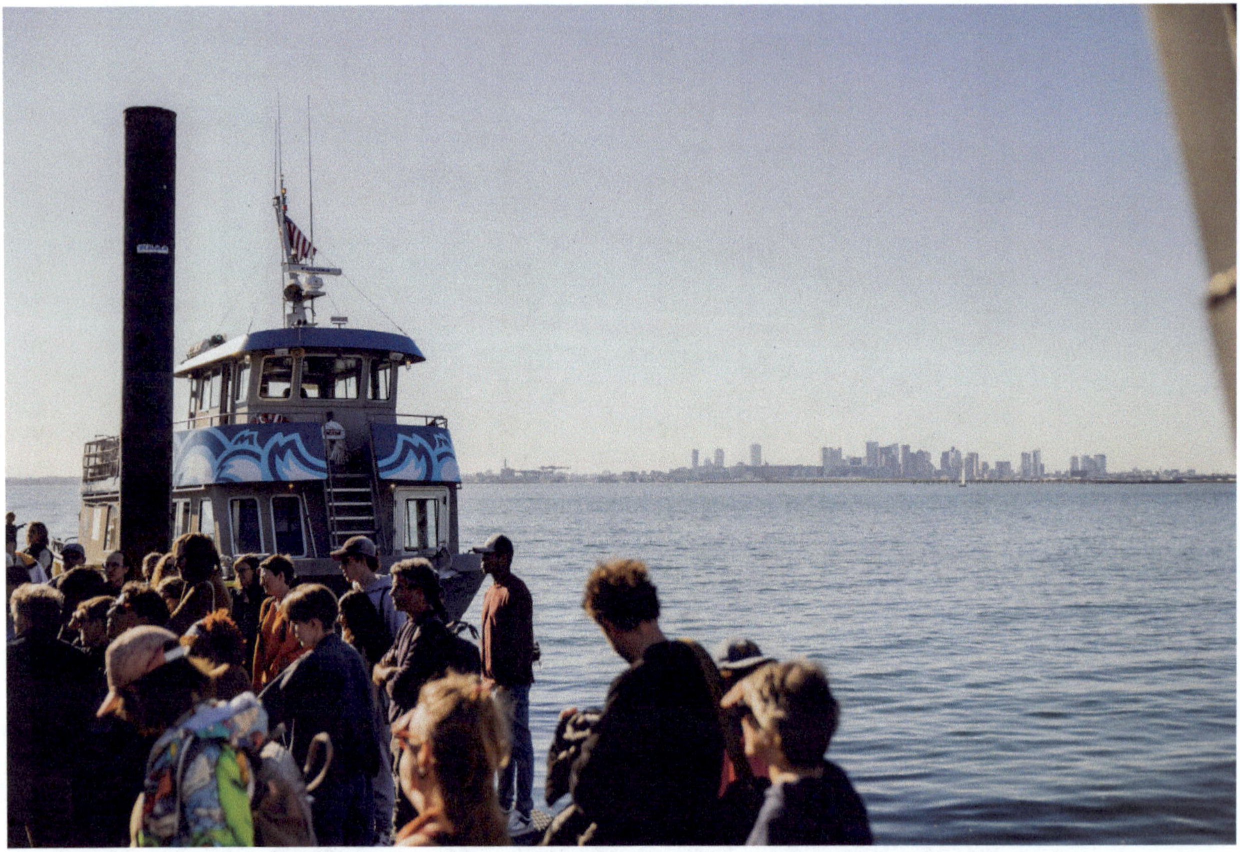

FIGURE 4.10 Passengers assemble on the boat dock during a stop on Deer Island, October 22, 2022. Photograph by Mel Taing

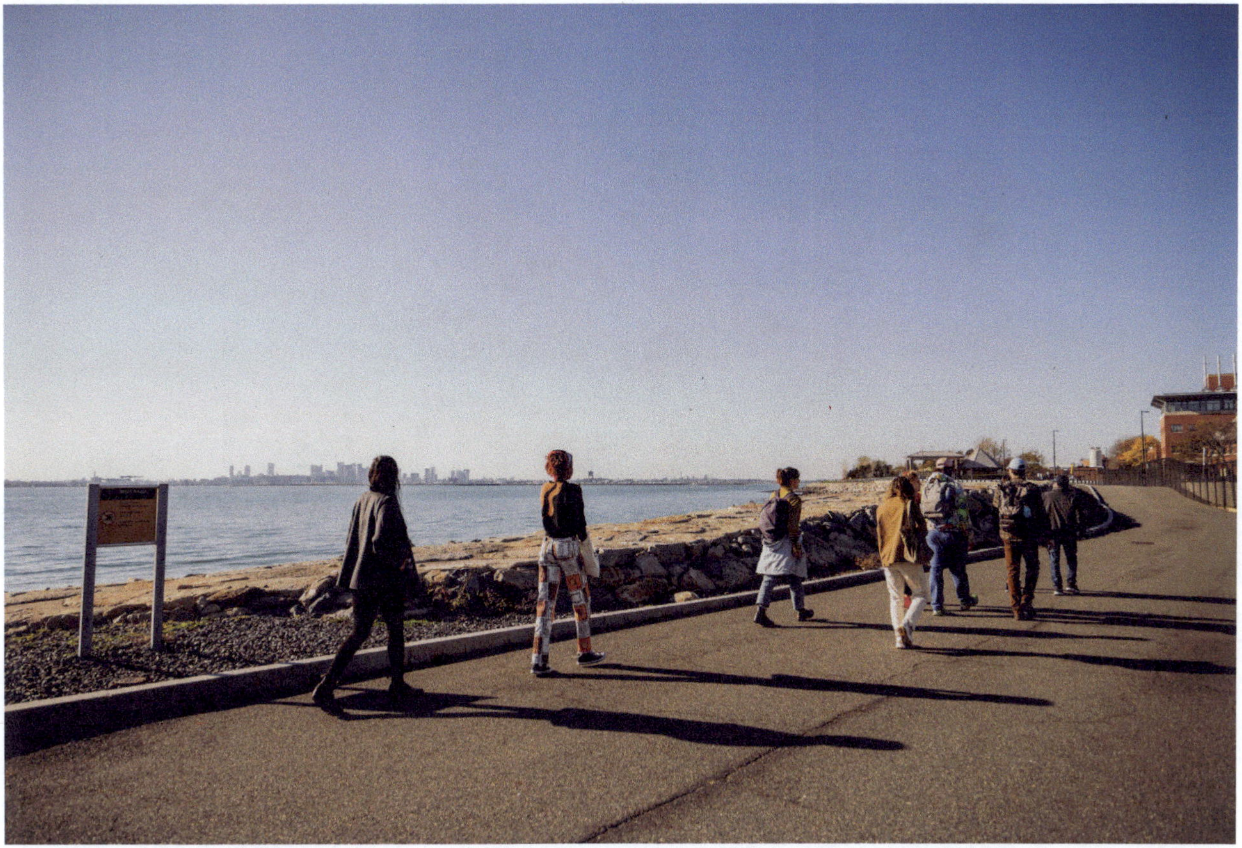

FIGURE 4.11 Participants in *Indigenous Boston Harbor* walk toward the Native American memorial site during a stop on Deer Island, October 22, 2022. Photograph by Mel Taing

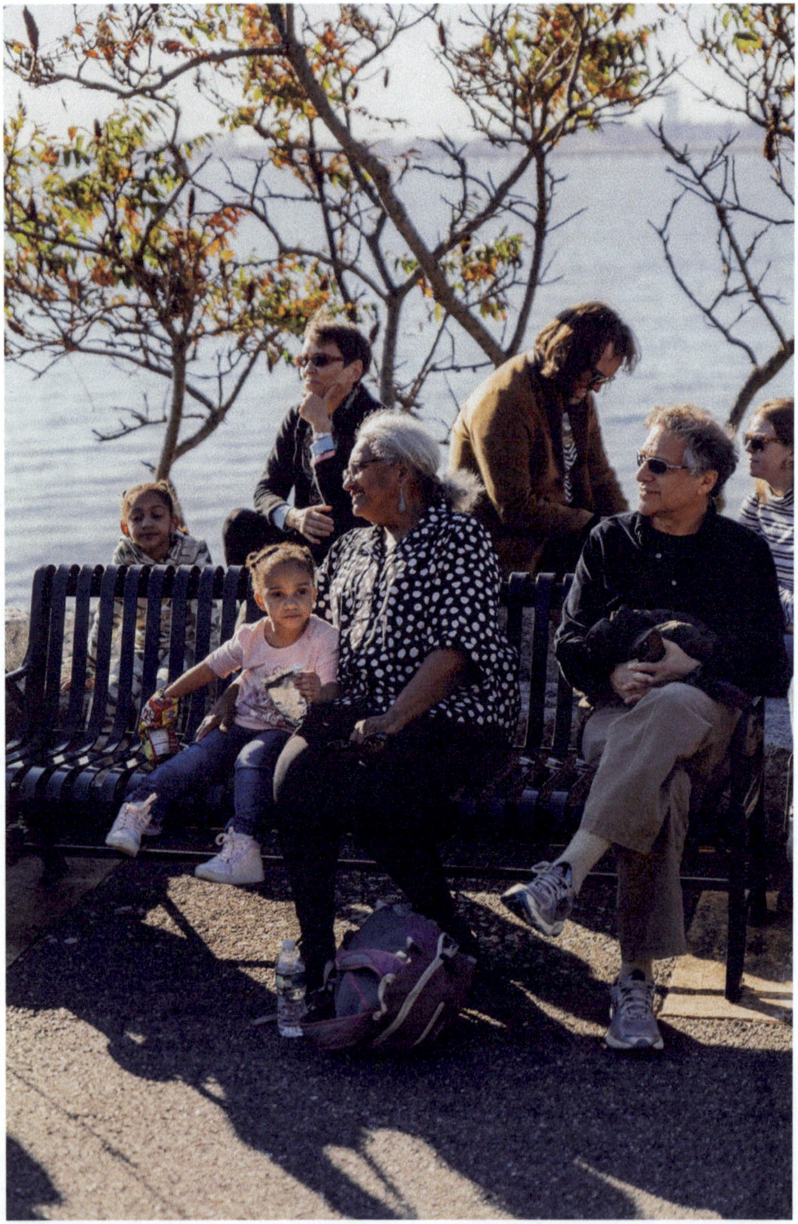

FIGURE 4.12 Elizabeth Solomon sits with Faries Gray's children during a stop at the Native American memorial site on Deer Island, October 22, 2022. Photograph by Mel Taing

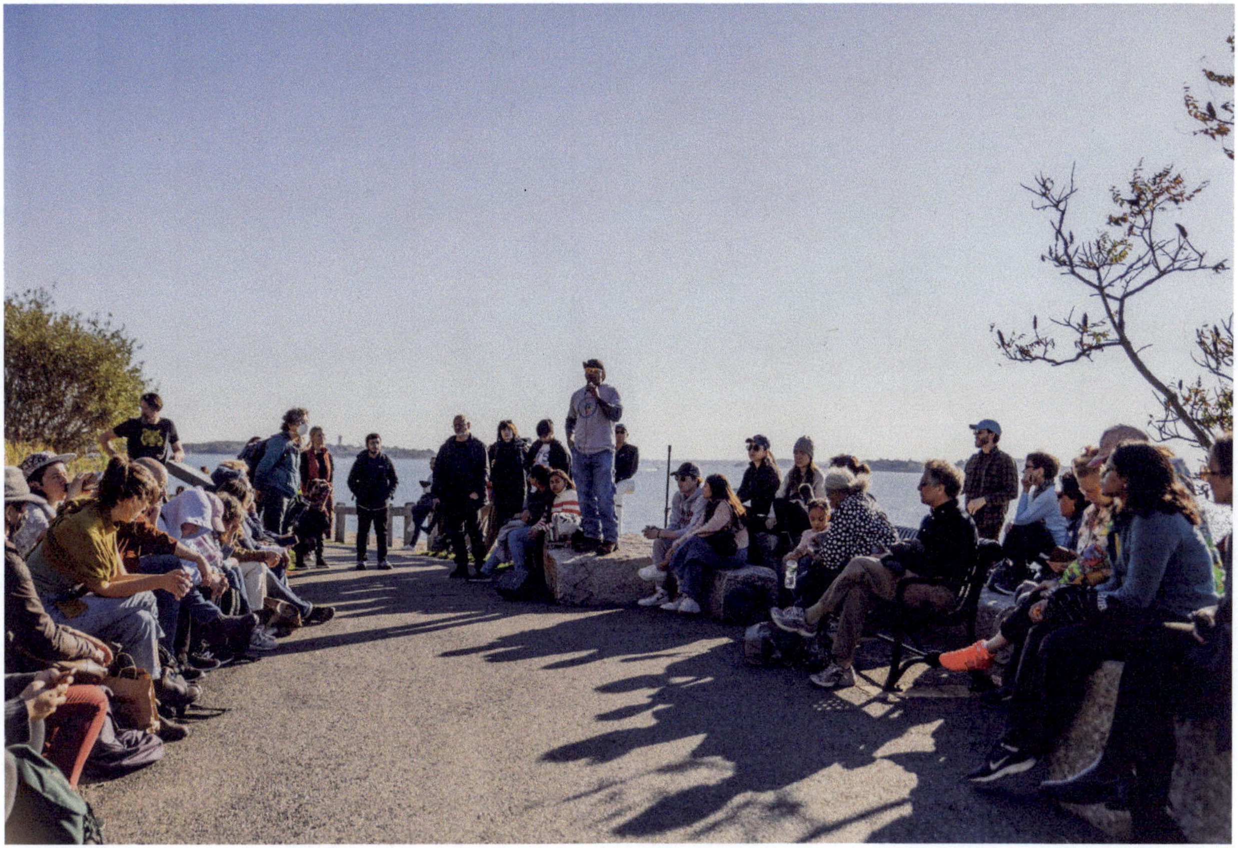

FIGURE 4.13 Faries Gray speaks to participants of *Indigenous Boston Harbor* at the Native American Memorial on Deer Island, October 22, 2022. Photograph by Mel Taing

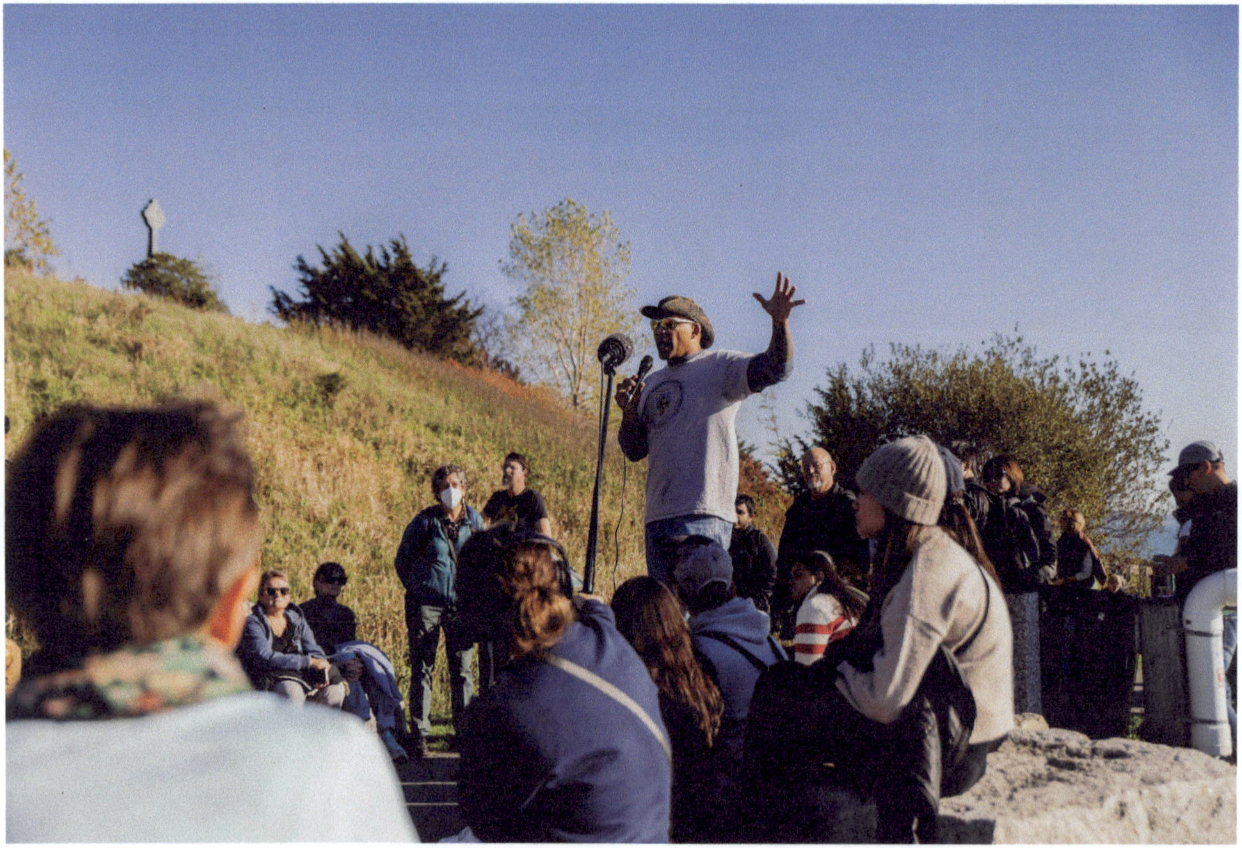

FIGURE 4.14 Faries Gray speaks to participants of *Indigenous Boston Harbor* at the Native American Memorial on Deer Island, October 22, 2022. The Celtic cross on the hill is the adjacent Irish Memorial. Photograph by Mel Taing

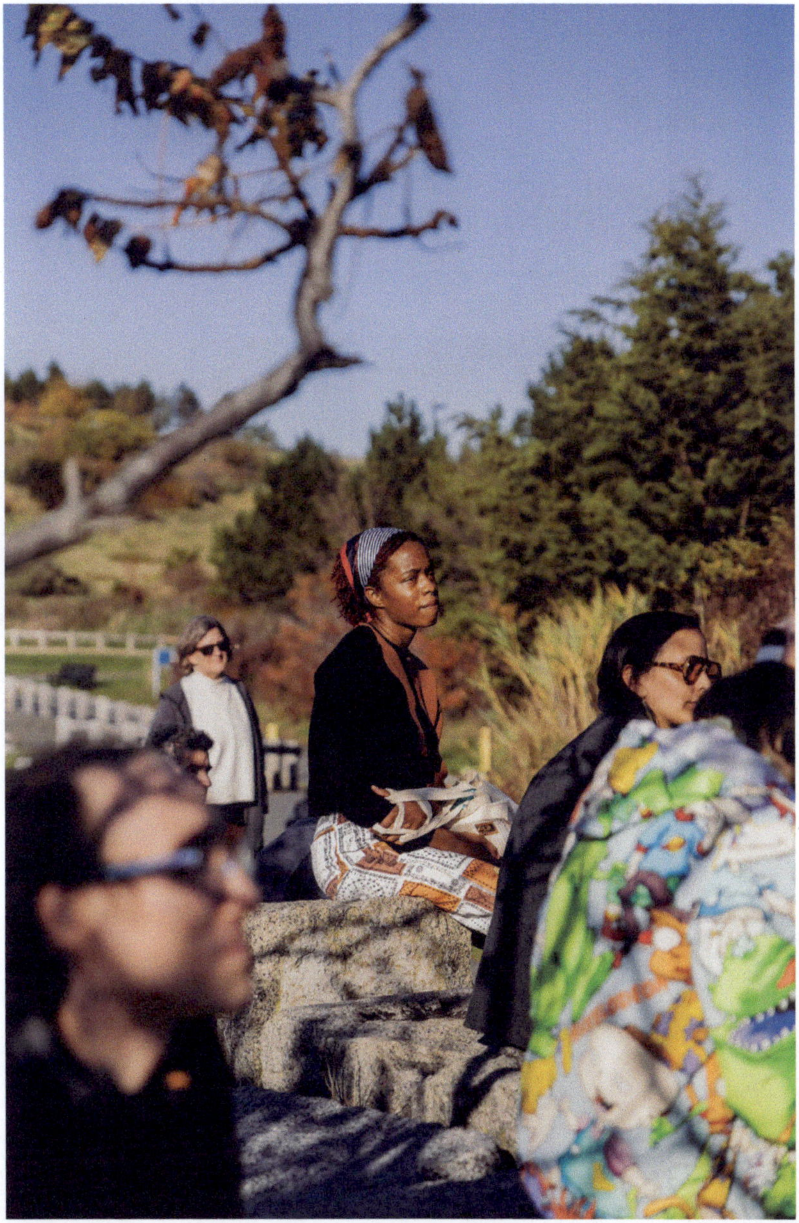

FIGURE 4.15 Participants in *Indigenous Boston Harbor* listen at the Native American Memorial on Deer Island, October 22, 2022. Photograph by Mel Taing

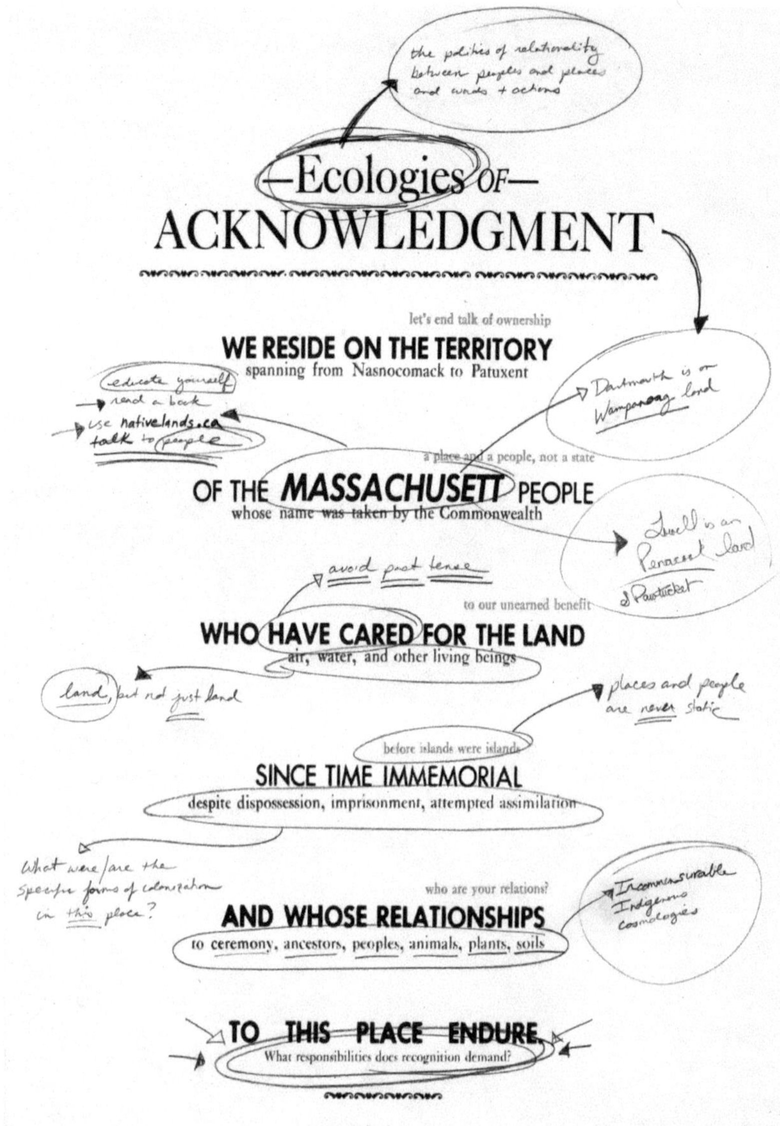

FIGURE 4.16 Sarah Kanouse and Nicholas Brown, *Ecologies of Acknowledgment*, 2019, Three-Color Letterpress Print, 12" x 19"

Kanouse and Brown created a downloadable and printable version of a letterpress print that was annotated over the course of three presentations in three different *Local Ecologies* exhibition sites. That print is available for free download at https://doi.org/10.3998/mpub.13189112.cmp.40

CHAPTER 5
Botanies of Migration

Duy Hoàng's *Vân Hà*—a proposed "library" of dried invasive plant species and other materials housed within an open-air structure—uses botany as both a metaphor and a concrete example to engage the politics of space. Human migrations define Massachusetts communities, and nonhuman animals and plants follow the global flows of human migrations. Some plant species are labeled "invasives," encapsulating the hostility with which migrant communities have been met. As of this writing, Hoàng's project has not been realized at UMass Lowell for reasons that demonstrate principles of conformity that govern campus landscaping. Diversity is central to the identity of the UMass Lowell community. Why then does conformity define our campus landscape? *Vân Hà* raises questions regarding what art is welcomed on a university campus and the unspoken rules that govern the use of public space.

VÂN HÀ AND THE COLLEGIATE PICTURESQUE

Duy Hoàng's *Vân Hà (Cloud River)* was commissioned by University of Massachusetts, Lowell to coincide with the *Local Ecologies* exhibition over the 2019–2020 academic year. Funding for the commission was provided by a grant from the Provost's Office awarded to introduce transdisciplinary programming around art and the environment. There was a great deal of support and excitement around bringing Hoàng and *Vân Hà* to campus. Hoàng, an alumnus of the UMass Lowell Art & Design Department, has received international attention for his investigations into the cultural meanings of landscape and nature through the lens of migration and displacement in his site-specific installations. The reflections introduced by his work seemed perfect for a campus that welcomes many first-generation college students and first-generation Americans, located in a city known for its vibrant immigrant communities.

Despite having secured funding and robust faculty support, *Vân Hà* remains unrealized in 2022. As the organizer who invited Hoàng to develop a public artwork, I ran into resistance relating to ways in which *Vân Hà* contravened institutional management of the campus grounds. Hoàng and I had initially hoped to site *Vân Hà* within a grove of mature oaks overlooking the Merrimack River adjacent to Allen House, an 1854 Italianate mansion that is the oldest building on campus. The proposed intention of *Vân Hà* was to reflect on natural history, human migrations, and acts of cultivation, and this site connected all these narratives. Views of the Merrimack evoke the mills that attracted generations of immigrants to Lowell, including Charles H. Allen, onetime resident of Allen House after whom the building is named. Allen was a prominent Massachusetts politician who served a brief term as Governor of Puerto Rico in 1900 before using his political connections to the island to start a vast sugar trading syndicate. *Vân Hà* invites participants to reflect on the global circulation of botanies and bodies through trade and migrations in the modern era. The chosen site next to Allen House connects *Vân Hà*'s concerns to broader histories of the sugar trade dependent on exploited labor that generated great wealth for European Americans with capital and connections in the nineteenth and early twentieth centuries.

We were discouraged from siting *Vân Hà* near Allen House because "this location is very visible from and proximate to the Allen House porch, which is a prime event location."[1] So why not display the work of a successful alumnus in this location? There were multiple concerns, including whether the structure filled with dead plants and loose papers would be legible as art, or would instead signal neglect. It was explained to me as curator that signs of neglect or lapsed maintenance would be problematic for Executive Cabinet members and inappropriate in proximity to a building used for fundraising and hosting prominent visitors. Yet the aesthetic of change and even loss were intentional. In an early conversation about *Vân Hà*, Hoàng and I had discussed entropy and the example of Robert Smithson's *Partially Buried Woodshed* (1970) on the campus of Kent State University. We both embraced the idea of an artwork weathering and becoming dilapidated with age, possibly collapsing into the earth. But evidence of entropy is generally unwelcome on a college campus where, like the landscaping itself, a public artwork is expected to align with institutional values.

In planning meetings assessing the viability of *Vân Hà*, members of the university administration expressed concerns over aesthetic impacts and messaging. It was important to Hoàng to site the library on grass. However, Facilities Management was discouraging: "the installation will likely kill the grass under it," which could not be "effectively restored until the following Spring."[2] An unsightly footprint of dead grass could be mitigated if *Vân Hà* were only installed from November through March, but this was a less-than-ideal solution given the New England climate. Beyond dead grass, the automated irrigation systems that operate from April to October would prevent the installation of *Vân Hà* on grass during these months as well.

Hoàng's preferred location adjacent to Allen House exacerbated aesthetic concerns given the building's use for high-profile events and fundraising activities.

At UMass Lowell, as on most campuses, a team of professional groundskeepers carefully selects plantings to reflect the university's mission. Bright annual blooms are timed to seasonal recruitment and graduation events. A small pollinator garden sponsored by the Office of Sustainability had been introduced in 2019 adjacent to Allen House. The garden looks wild in the tradition of the picturesque garden—but the wildflowers introduced in the pollinator garden have been carefully selected and a website (now archived) introduces each species.[3] Almost all of European origin—a cultivated ethnocentrism. In an early version of *Vân Hà*, Hoàng proposed the inclusion of both invasive and native dried plant species as part of an open-air library. The seeds would gradually disperse over months as breezes passed through the structure and carried away bits of organic matter—the plants and pages weighted down but not fully secured to allow this natural material migration. Those determined to be "invasives" are, of course, "weeds." Their circulation tends to correspond with trade and human migrations. Unlike the cultivated wildflowers of the pollinator garden, many so-called invasives originate in Asia.

As a means of unruly dispersal of (unwanted) invasive plant species across irrigated, fertilized, weeded grounds, *Vân Hà* would disrupt a specific vision of cultivated open green space. As part of an institutional commitment to sustainability and accessibility, UMass Lowell reimagined its South Campus landscape with a mission "to create a welcoming environment that allows students to relax, rejuvenate, and strengthen bonds between each other and nature."[4] A Boston-based landscape architecture firm, Crosby | Schlesinger | Smallridge (CSS), was hired in 2018 to design a master plan for South Campus focused on these principles, with the goal "to create a heart for South Campus."[5] The CSS vision focused on open spaces—expansive lawns highlighted by deciduous trees. A montage generated by the firm depicts a collegiate picturesque. Students socialize and recreate on perfect sod lined with a uniform row of young trees, offset by a single mature shade tree in peak New England fall foliage. Not a weed has sprouted, nor a leaf fallen into this digital idyll—a perpetually maintained, constantly renewed *image* of landscape. The unnatural, uncanny coherence of this image conceals the contested origins of a landscape that, as with all landscape, is formed of conflict and mechanisms of exclusion.

Vân Hà offers instead landscape as text and materiality to be read, touched, and explored. Hoàng's research would reveal a complex, even incoherent, narrative of nature and landscape in Lowell that is still in the process of being written. *Vân Hà* proposes landscape shaped by a multiplicity of agents—one that renders legible multiple histories, personal and individual; responds to global migration and exchange; and possesses an agency outside of human groundskeepers.

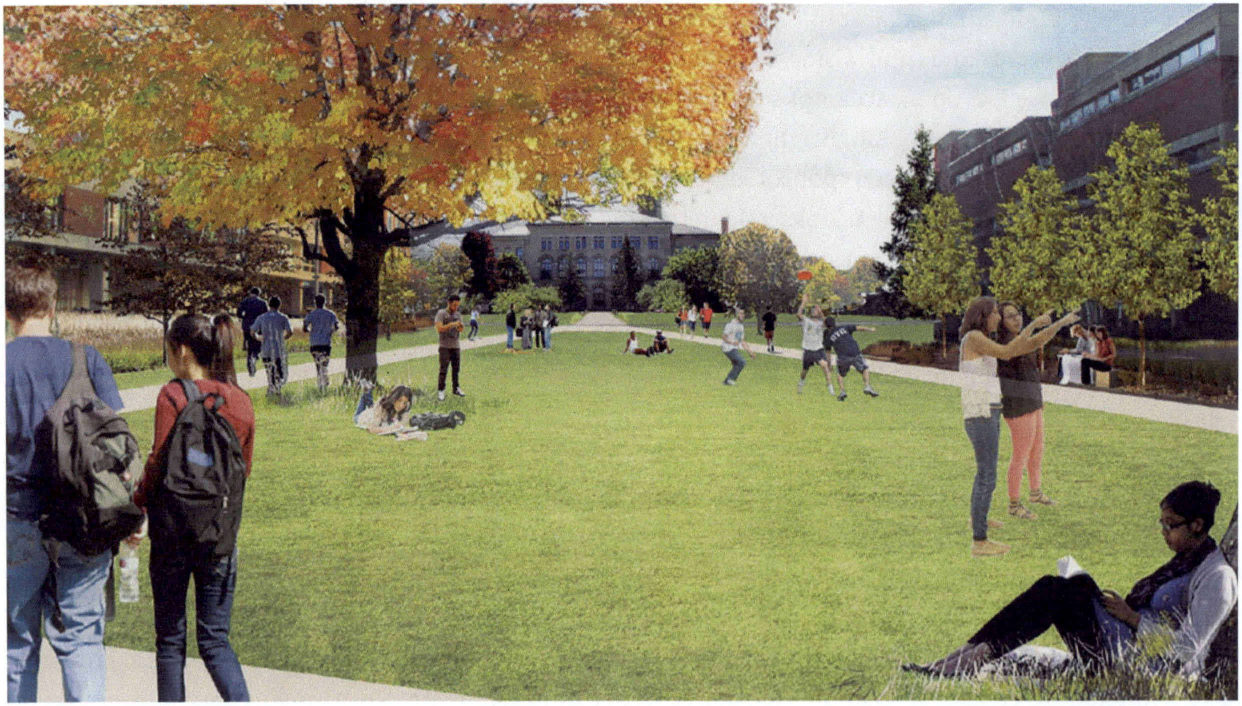

FIGURE 5.1 UMass Lowell South Campus master plan mockup by firm Crosby | Schlessinger | Smallridge, 2016

VÂN HÀ (CLOUD RIVER)

Duy Hoàng

Vân Hà (Cloud River) is a mixed-media public artwork installation proposed for the campus of the University of Massachusetts, Lowell by Duy Hoàng. Hoàng's project statement is as follows:

Vân Hà (Cloud River) investigates the need for attentiveness to our immediate surroundings, revealing the nuances of everyday life within the vast habitat we occupy and far beyond. Through research of native and invasive species of the Eastern Massachusetts region, I want to emphasize the notion of migration/immigration within our ecologies, both natural and political. This endeavor collapses our local boundaries that expand to the rest of the world.

Vân Hà (Cloud River) adopts the form of a solarium structure with a collection of natural and research materials displayed within, situated upon a South Campus hilltop overlooking the Merrimack River. Much like a greenhouse, the structure is constructed out of wood and covered with polycarbonate sheeting all around. The transparent quality of the polycarbonate material highlights the voyeuristic and exposed characteristics of a private collection and the act of research. The accumulated natural materials presented inside are to be gathered from the surrounding areas that represent a sample of native plant species in Eastern Massachusetts. Entwined with these natural materials is an evolving collection of observational drawings, documentary format photographs, screen printing, digital prints, found objects, etc., that represent invasive species found in this region. These specimens will be analyzed and mapped to consider their origins, causes for migration, and effects on the environments they occupy. Beyond this scientific treatment, the concept of migration ties to my personal history as an immigrant and reflects the consequences of human behaviors in shaping natural and human history.

This project stems from my ongoing research into “home” and site-responsive adaptation behaviors. I constantly recall my moment of migration to the United States at a young age. The transition demanded my intensive observation and awareness in order to comprehend the new foreign habitat. Consequently, my practice focuses on our relationships to the minutia around us in connection to the much larger environment, while searching for our place within that spectrum. With this desire for attentiveness, my practice dissects the surrounding location, accumulates site-specific found natural materials that are often overlooked, then applies observational processes to highlight their significance within the larger ecosystem. This practice grows into a “nesting” process, which embodies an obsessive impulse to investigate the construct of “home” and pursue an understanding of our symbiotic relationships with our local ecology.

In particular, I want to take a closer look at our relationship to the location of Lowell, Massachusetts—to discover webs of connection to our surroundings at large. *Vân Hà (Cloud River)* is a space where viewers are able to participate in the act of observation and attentiveness to the space we are occupying and the nuances of moments in our walks of life. These moments link to each other, thus constructing an elaborate symbiotic ecosystem of its own. The ecology expands from human to the environment, organic to artificial, natural to spiritual, physical to conceptual, and so on.

Similar to the solarium as a treatment for liver diseases or greenhouse nursery for ill plants, *Vân Hà (Cloud River)* investigates the observation of decay, processes of preservation, memory documentation, and the archive. In turn, we can learn to deal with death, preserve lives/memories, and invigorate a new cycle of growth. The exploratory nature of *Vân Hà (Cloud River)* hopes to connect us to the history of our place, time, and matter, while reexamining our philosophical ways of being with one another.

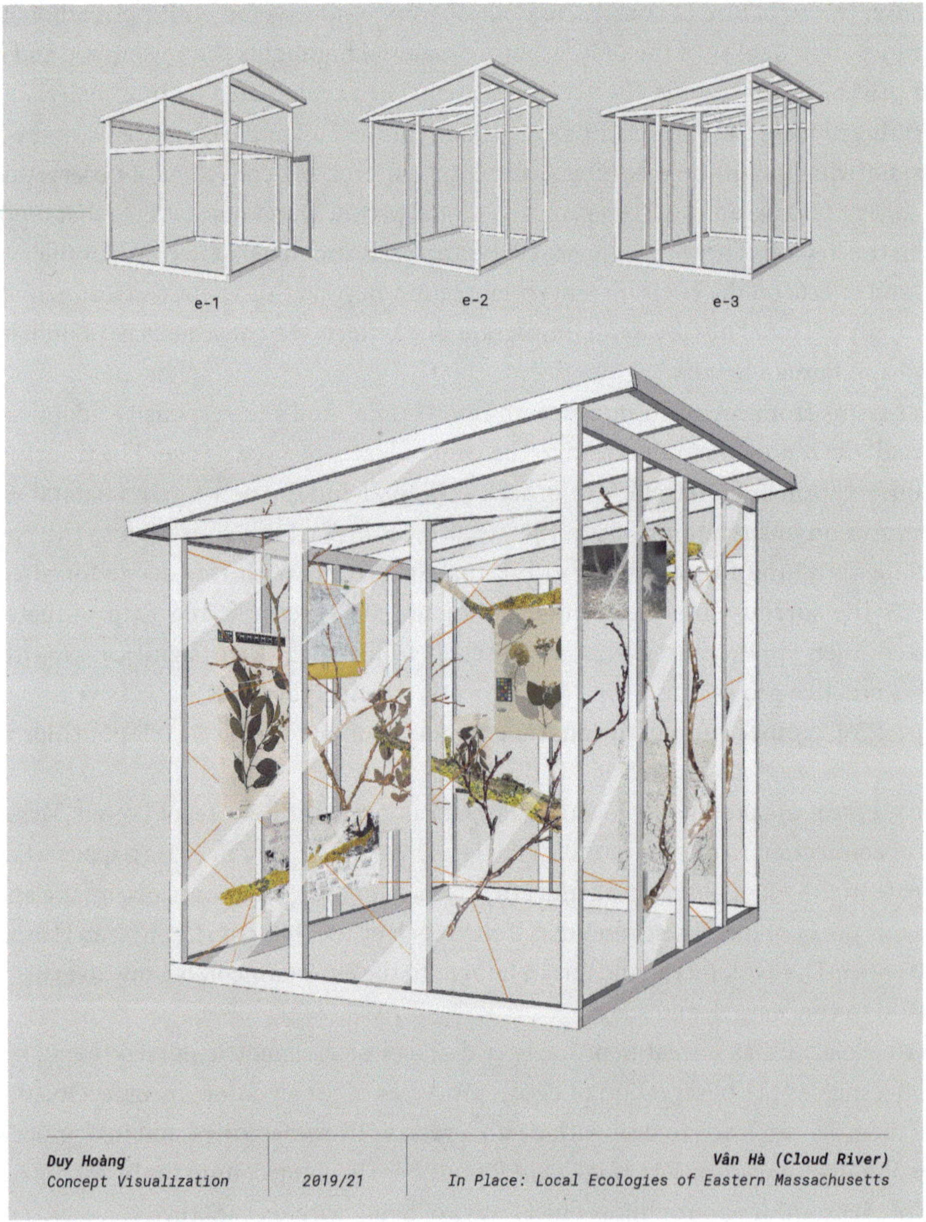

FIGURE 5.2 Duy Hoàng, concept visualization for *Vân Hà (Cloud River)*, 2019

CHAPTER 6
Ground Truthing

Ground truth is a term used to describe verified observable information, measured in the world. Artist Dan Borelli refers to this term and process when thinking about the interpretive and experiential limits and activities that inscribe a place. In this chapter, Borelli, artist María Magdalena Campos-Pons, and National Park Service Ranger Andrew Schnetzer present their contributions to the *Local Ecologies* exhibition. Together, their work investigates truths on the ground, focused particularly on themes of monumentality and memory. Who are the stewards of our historical and environmental stories? Whose stories are told by whom, and how?

ICONIC GESTURES

For this volume, we have produced a series of video roundtable discussions. This roundtable convened National Park Service (NPS) Ranger Andy Schnetzer, artists María Magdelena Campos-Pons and Dan Borelli, and art historian/curator (and *Local Ecologies* coeditor) Rebecca Uchill, to discuss themes of sedimentary layers of history that stand behind the participants' research, activism, art, and educational work.

Over the course of a spring 2019 residency with the New Bedford Whaling National Historical Park (NHP), artist Dan Borelli made a series of investigations into the Superfund site of New Bedford Harbor, one of the most contaminated sites identified for Environmental Protection Agency (EPA) cleanup. The seafloor of the harbor retains pollution produced by local electronics manufacturers using polychlorinated biphenyls (PCBs) before they were prohibited by the EPA, and most fish caught in the harbor remain unsafe to eat. Borelli invited local audiences to address New Bedford's harbor contamination through dialogue and cognitive mapping. Following his poetic research forms, including reading Herman Melville's writings, painting harbor views, exploring civic histories, and documenting residents' reactions and imaginations in response

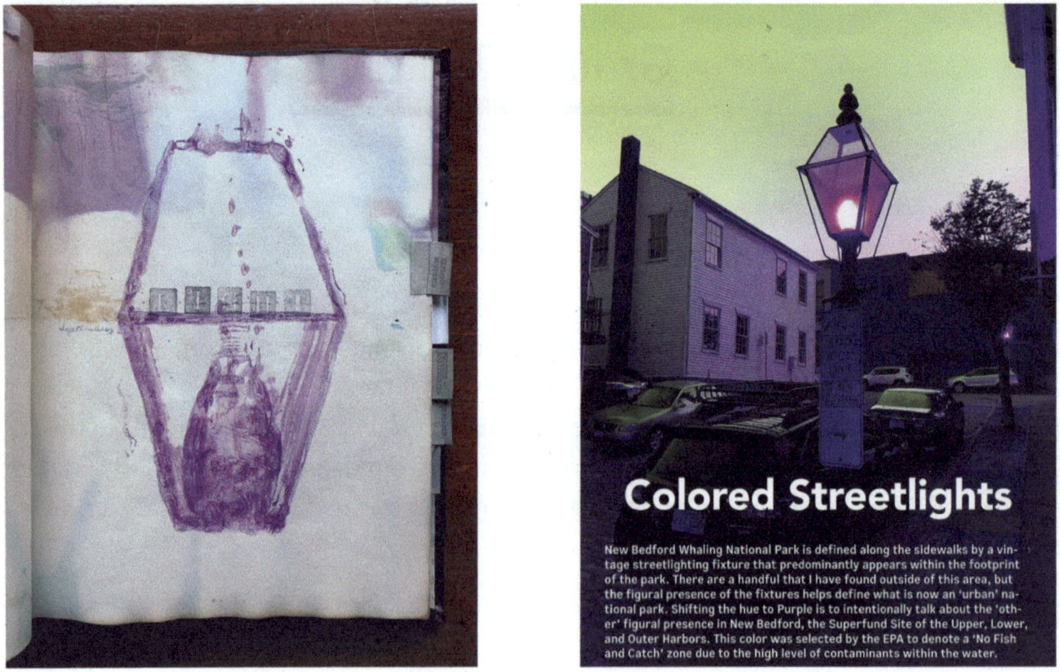

FIGURE 6.1 Dan Borelli, "Colored Streetlights" from *Proposals for the City of New Bedford*, 2019

to the sources and locations of hazardous waste, the artist proposed a series of potential public art projects responding to community reactions to the Superfund imaginary.[1]

Lucem Diffundo, the Latin motto of the City of New Bedford, which also appears on its seal, translates to "I diffuse light." Borelli's public art proposals—developed during his 2018 artist residency with the National Park Service—make use of light to chart experiences of the contamination of the Upper, Lower, and Outer Harbor. One proposal, for example, involves streetlamps on New Bedford sidewalks; another places solar-powered illuminated buoys on harbor waters to chart the EPA's "diagrammatic boundary of environmental impact."[2]

Another example of the rich poesis artists brought to interpretations of "local ecologies" is seen in the artwork of María Magdalena Campos-Pons. Campos-Pons connects the conditions of the "local" to "global" enterprise

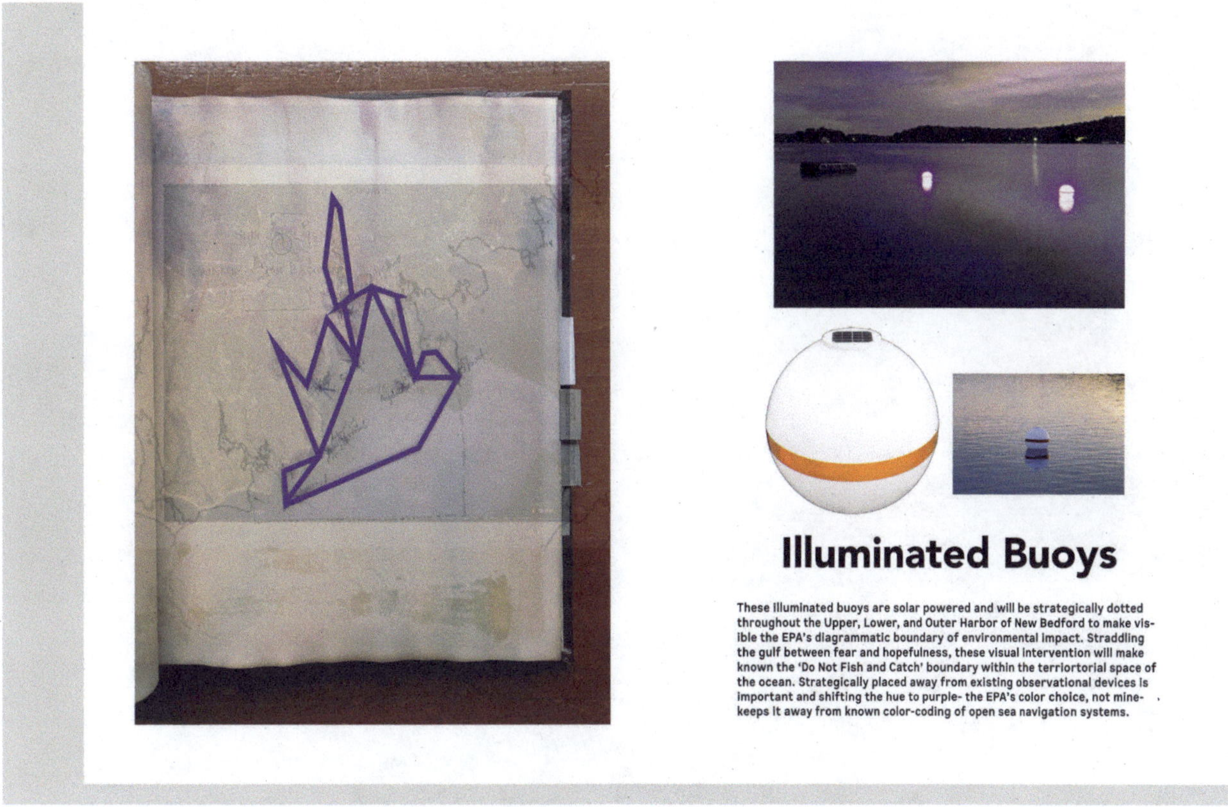

FIGURE 6.2 Dan Borelli, "Illuminated Buoys" from *Proposals for the City of New Bedford*, 2019

through her consideration of trans-oceanic commercial transactions that had substantial material consequences for local livelihoods. Her installation *19/19 Molasses Intervals*, with two related drawings in gold ink and molasses, focuses on complex histories of labor and race that also characterized the artist's own experience with family and homeland. Campos-Pons emigrated to Boston, where she lived for many years, from Matanzas, Cuba, where she grew up in a former slave barracks on a sugar plantation. The city of Matanzas historically exported sugar-based products such as rum to port cities, including those in Massachusetts. The artwork points to those trade conditions and their associating turbulent histories of labor, racial prejudice, and lapses in industrial regulation (such as the history of Boston's Great Molasses Flood of 1919). For years, sugar has been a repeated motif in the artist's work, where the material has come to characterize health, transit, labor, exportation, and exploitation.

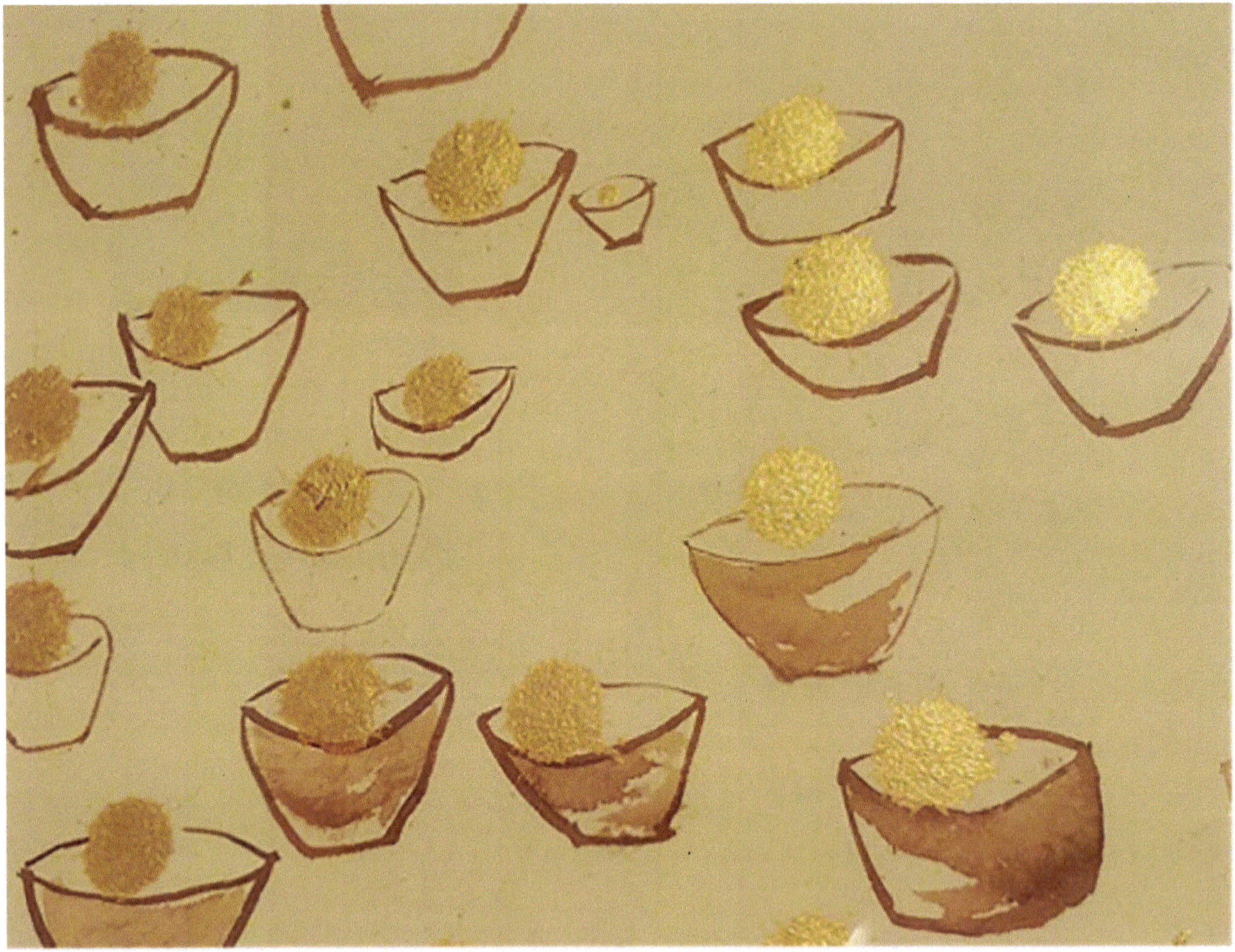

FIGURE 6.3 María Magdalena Campos-Pons, *Cleaning the Spills*, 2019, detail

As she relayed in an interview in September 2019, "[Even] in my hate towards sugar—I have a lot of hate towards sugar—I love that sugar preserves things, like salt and vinegar. Excess of sugar in the blood will kill you, but sugar is a fundamental marker and barometer of your life options and capacity."[3]

Together these projects allow us to consider the entanglements of global and local histories of place, rendering tangible and sensory crises of capitalist violence and myths of nationalism. This discussion focused on the sedimentary layers of both ground and of history that these projects connote: Campos-Pons's project connects the Atlantic sugar trade with the mutualities of the export industry that brought Northeastern

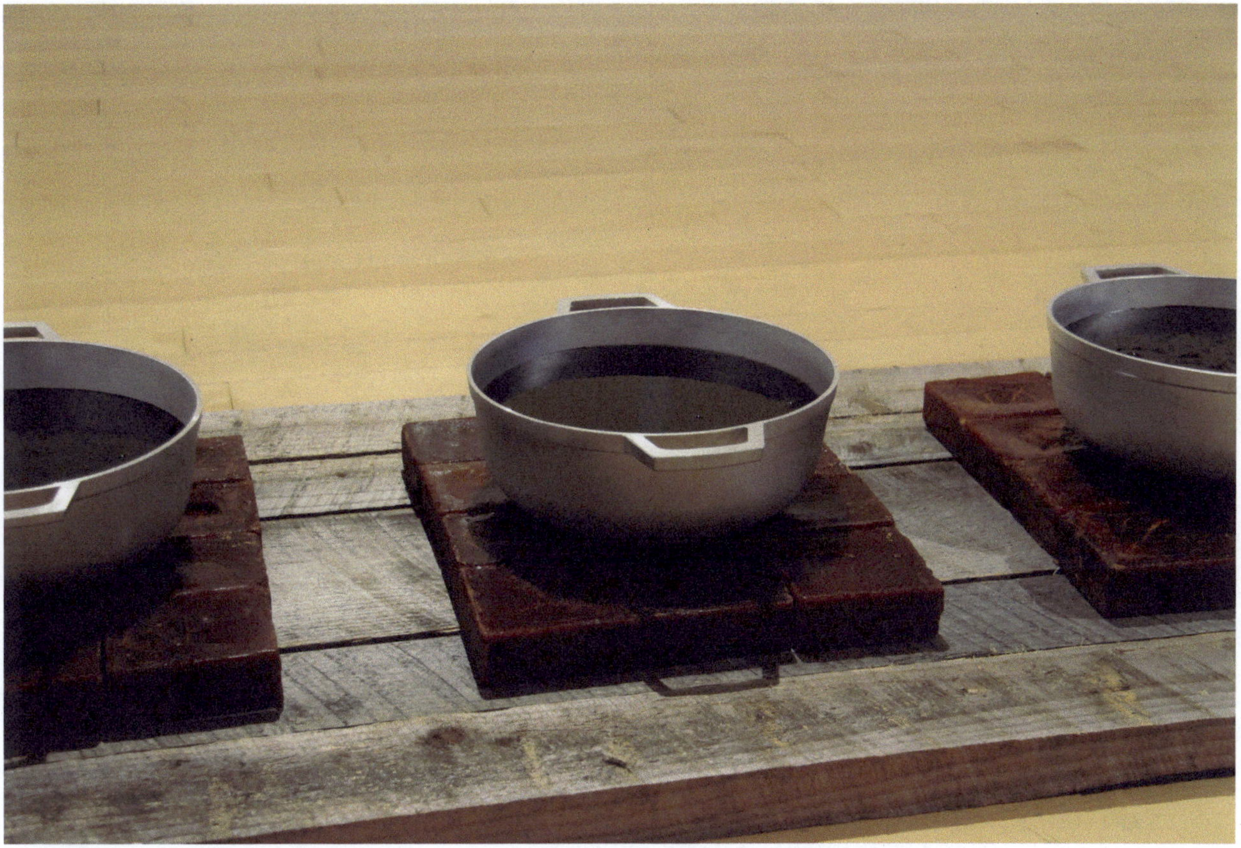

FIGURE 6.4 María Magdalena Campos-Pons, *19/19 Molasses Intervals,* 2019, detail

United States stones back to line the groundwork of the streets of the city. Borelli's NPS residency project investigates the toxicities underfoot in the Superfund site of New Bedford through the consideration of groundwater and the relationship of the town to the harbor. His installation artwork refers to a geological object—a rock—that is loaded with signification in being cast as a monument to colonial enterprise. The conversation was joined by a Park Ranger, Andy Schnetzer, who spoke with the artists about the role of the institution of the NPS in its claims of protecting and interpreting bounded parcels of land. Schnetzer was involved in organizing the residency program that brought Borelli's project to New Bedford.

On March 25, 2021, Borelli, Campos-Pons, and Schnetzer recorded a video conversation about the sedimentary layers of histories that ground their research, activism, art, and educational work. This roundtable video is available at: https://doi.org/10.3998/mpub.13189112.cmp.47

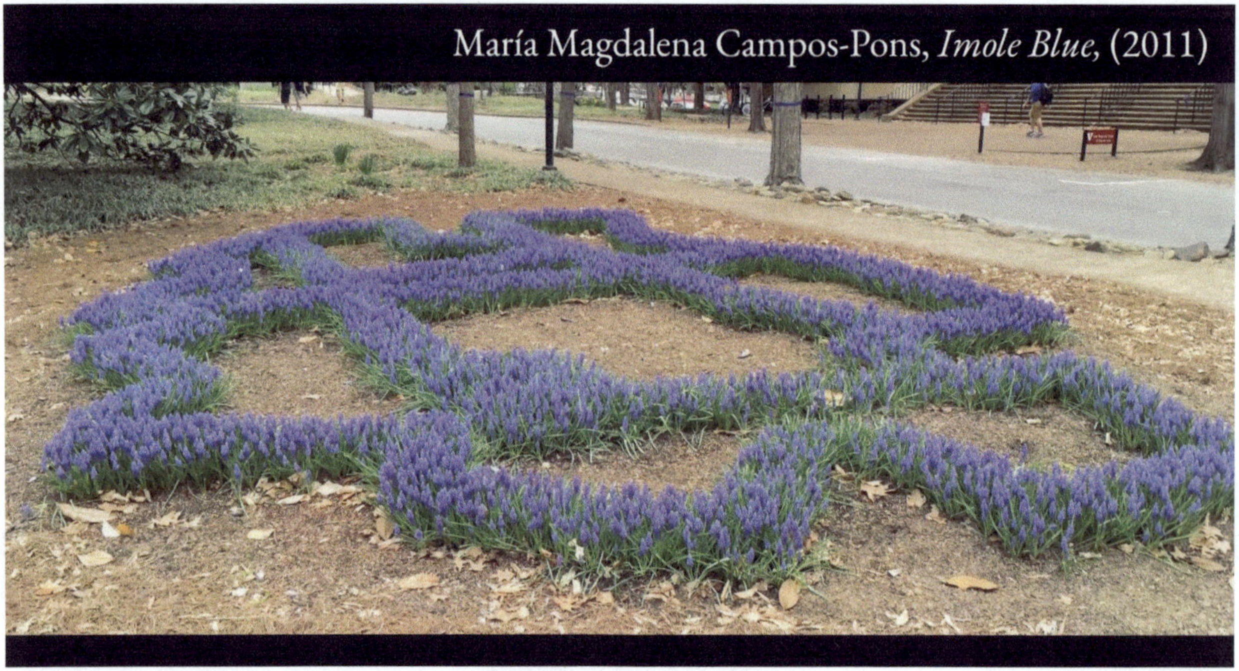

FIGURE 6.5 Still image from *Ground Truthing* roundtable video

NOTES ON DAN BORELLI'S RESIDENCY

National Park Service Ranger Andrew Schnetzer

The artist-in-residence program at New Bedford Whaling NHP was established to amplify the voices of steward partners of the national park site. A multiyear project set in what was the new Corson MakerSpace, the artist-in-residence program began in the late fall of 2017 and continues through the time of this writing in 2023. In the summer of 2018, artist Dan Borelli held a three-month residency that focused on the history of industrial pollution of the New Bedford Harbor (a Superfund mega-site) and the cleanup efforts by the EPA. He was selected by the park for his articulate stance on environmental justice, his catalog of outstanding public engagement on the topic of environmental justice, and clear proposal for meaningful interpretation of the site.

The role of the NPS during Dan Borelli's residency was to create a welcoming space to work, a platform for him to engage with residents and park visitors, and an opportunity for national reach of his work. Park staff made introductions throughout the local arts and culture community and offered opportunities for

Dan to present his work, which centered on the experiences of people who lived through many of the changes he explored. The community members he interviewed recalled places that were part of the industrial landscape of New Bedford but have now been repurposed or are utilized differently. Working in the Corson MakerSpace studio and in a mobile studio within the historical park boundary, Borelli facilitated deep and meaningful conversations with members of this community as a partner of the NPS. Layers of this dynamic industrial ecology revealed themselves as Dan continued to dig into the unrepresented past. He articulated how his practice delicately responded to the themes and intensity of his conversations. As you can see in his artist book, the experiences shared during his interviews resulted in a blending of his own lived experience and those of the community he engaged with.

As it happens, the EPA uses the same NPS facility as a meeting space to hold public Q&A sessions about the status of the Superfund site cleanup. In a culminating moment, Borelli was present as an independent artist, the park's artist in residence, and public advocate as he participated in dialogue about the status of the cleanup and the experience of those affected by the pollution. What might seem to have been a potentially tense exchange turned out to demonstrate remarkable common ground. Dan's questions about the status of the cleanup and the potential for declaring the cleanup over demonstrated that these stakeholders shared a mutual concern for public health and accountability for public safety. It showed that an activist artist and the EPA were hoping for a very similar outcome: a healthy and safe harbor. His artist book reflects the specific places and times relevant to this story while also conveying a theme which has shrouded New Bedford since its founding—that environmental justice is woven into the fabric of all social justice.

The effects of his time in the National Historical Park continued beyond his tenure as artist in residence. In March of 2020, Dan Borelli, Andrew Schnetzer, and New Bedford Whaling NHP public engagement program manager Joshua Boles presented at the national Public Lands Alliance conference in Washington, DC. Their presentation utilized Dan's residency as an example of the powerful outcomes possible when taking calculated risks in the public engagement work of the NPS. They presented the framework of the Corson MakerSpace and artist-in-residence program as a formal method of overcoming the risk-averse tendencies of an agency whose mission is to inspire stewardship for public lands.

Meanwhile, the artist-in-residence program at New Bedford Whaling NHP continues to thrive, engaging a wide spectrum of voices, perspectives, media, and themes.

Editors' note: This essay was written by Ranger Andy Schnetzer in 2023, as a reflection on the vital artist residency program at the New Bedford Whaling NHP. As of today, in March 2025, the residency program continues.

Dan Borelli's artist book was produced during his NPS residency in New Bedford. *The Whiteness of the Whale* tells the story of the local landscapes in New Bedford and how we can reimagine the spatial network of Superfund sites. It is included in full here: https://doi.org/10.3998/mpub.13189112.cmp.48

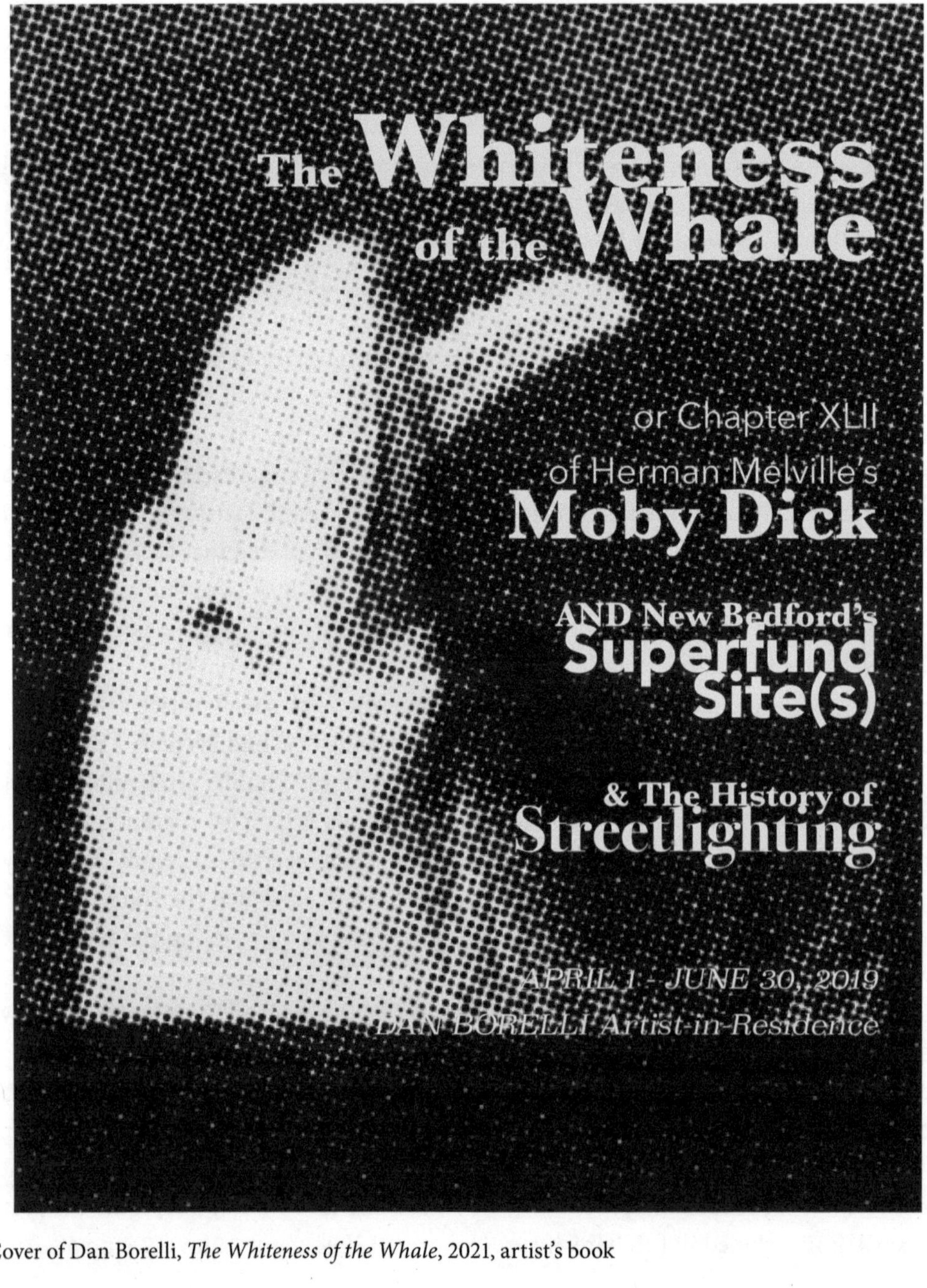

FIGURE 6.6 Cover of Dan Borelli, *The Whiteness of the Whale*, 2021, artist's book

CHAPTER 7
Life of the Merrimack

The health of our bodies depends on the health of our local ecologies. Evelyn Rydz and Andrew S. Yang focus on the Merrimack River ecosystem, bringing focus to levels of pollution in the river that flows through postindustrial mill towns in New Hampshire and Massachusetts—and also flows through our taps and our mouths. Here, ecology is not a metaphor but a material condition of interdependence. The river's health is critical to the wellbeing of countless plant and animal species. To care for the river is to care for our bodies.

The roundtable video included in this volume, titled *Global Flows*, was recorded on April 16, 2021, and it spanned an hour of conversation about the global circulation of water. Rydz and Yang's conversation is available at: https://doi.org/10.3998/mpub.13189112.cmp.49

In Lowell, an important focus of *Local Ecologies* was the Merrimack River, a site where social, political, industrial, and natural systems converge. The river powered the Industrial Revolution and is the reason UMass Lowell is here today. Yet the huge factories along its banks, from Manchester to Lawrence, destroyed the river's ecosystems. As Thoreau wrote in 1849, "Salmon, Shad, and Alewives were formerly abundant here, and taken in weirs by the Indians, who taught this method to the whites…until the dam, and afterward the canal at Billerica, and the factories at Lowell, put an end their migrations hitherward."[1] Toxic runoff and sewage overflow continue to seriously compromise the Merrimack, even as the river provides water to over half a million residents of the Merrimack Valley.

Evelyn Rydz's installation *The Mouth: A Merrimack River Project* addressed the status of the river today. The artist arranged 500 used water glasses on the gallery floor to form a map of the Merrimack, from the New Hampshire border to the river's "mouth" at Newburyport. Cement pavers used in the installation evoke the dam, the built environment, and the impervious parking lots and roads along the river's course that

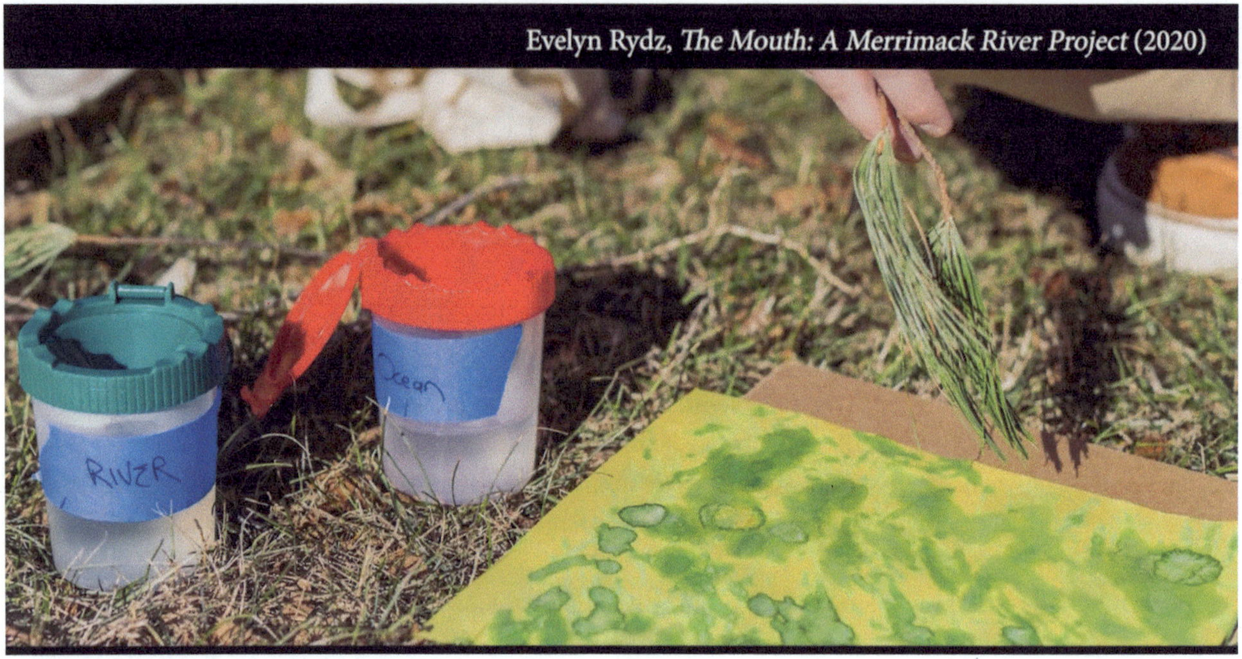

FIGURE 7.1 Still image from *Global Flows* roundtable video, produced for *Local Ecologies*, 2025

create runoff. The glasses were filled with water gathered from the banks of the Merrimack. This contained plastic and Styrofoam debris, seeds, and other organic and inorganic matter. Though the water was dingy and polluted, over the course of the exhibition seedlings grew from the river water. We felt despair as the Trump administration announced rollbacks of the Clean Water Act during the course of Rydz's installation. But the seedlings offered a tiny hint of resilience.

Rydz also invited the public to make paintings on pH paper using water collected at the banks of the Merrimack River in Lowell as well as at the mouth of the Merrimack at Plum Island, near Newburyport. Here, the Merrimack empties into the Atlantic Ocean, carrying our local effluences into the global current. Groups of visitors and students used natural materials gathered from the landscape—pine needles, sticks, dried grass—to paint with water. We looked out at the river as we painted, considering both the idea of landscape as a visual experience and as a space of being where we smell the earth and touch the water. The pH paper changed to slightly different colors depending on whether one painted with local river water, ocean water, or a combination. This

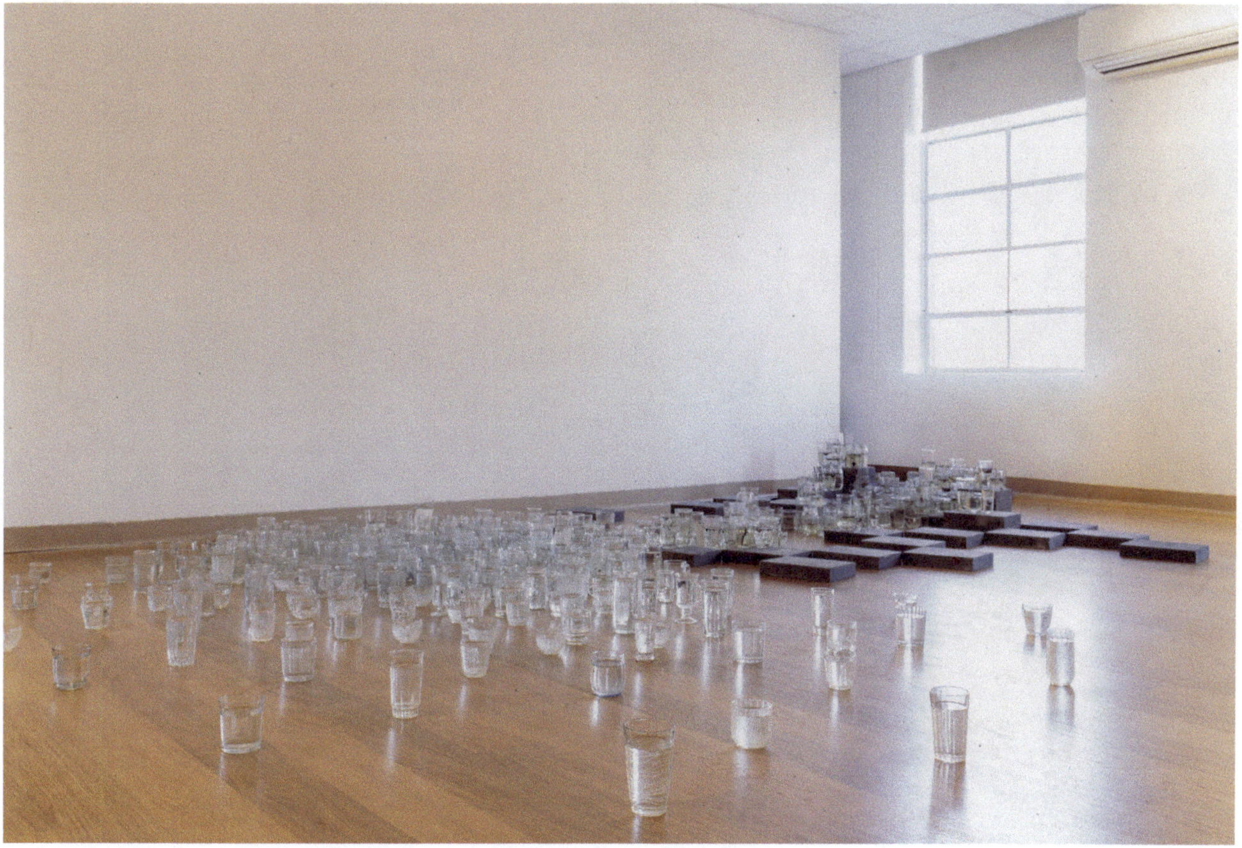

FIGURE 7.2 Evelyn Rydz, *The Mouth: A Merrimack River Project,* 2020. Photo: Mel Taing

creative sensory engagement encouraged us to reflect on water as a specific chemical substance on which our bodies depend, while simultaneously seeing water within an ecosystem and a landscape.

The artist Andrew S. Yang created an installation for the UMass Lowell campus entitled *Waste Knot, Want Knot* (2019), engaging with the history of plastics in the region. In the early twentieth century, Eastern Massachusetts companies pioneered the mass production of plastics, from Tupperware to combs. Today, these mass-produced plastics contribute to an environmental crisis of staggering proportions. Yang installed snake-shaped banners made from waste plastics in the university's libraries, evoking the "good and evil" conflict of plastics consumption.

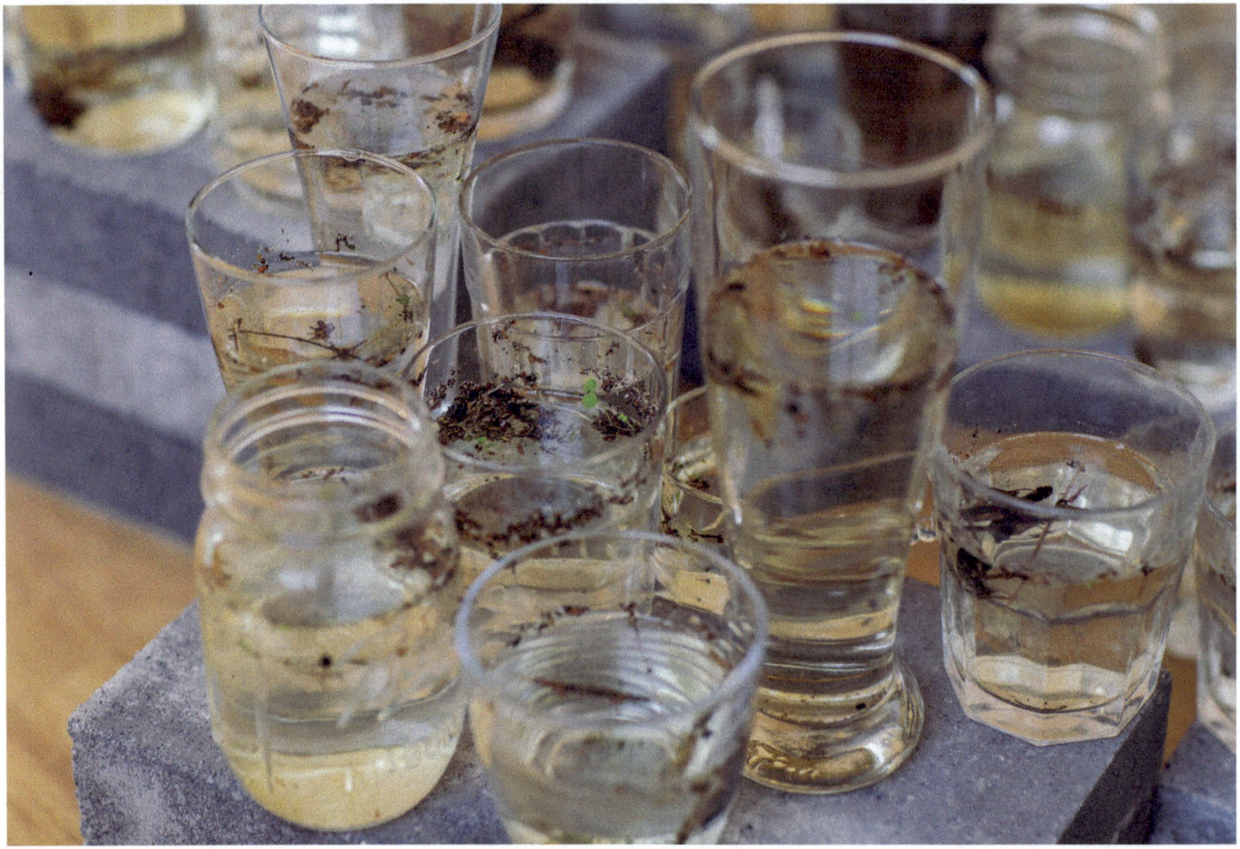

FIGURE 7.3 Evelyn Rydz, *The Mouth: A Merrimack River Project,* 2020, detail. Photo: Mel Taing

In the gallery, Yang assembled curio shelves with numerous artifacts representing plastic's various forms and uses. He gathered raw plastic "nurdles"—tiny pellets melted for the injection-molding process—during visits to plastics factories in Leominster. Blobs and strands of plastic "purge," a byproduct of injection molding, were gathered from a plastics engineering lab on the UMass Lowell campus. In the lab, Yang injected an experimental bioplastic into plastic brush-handle molds from the first half of the twentieth century, creating objects that merge these material histories.

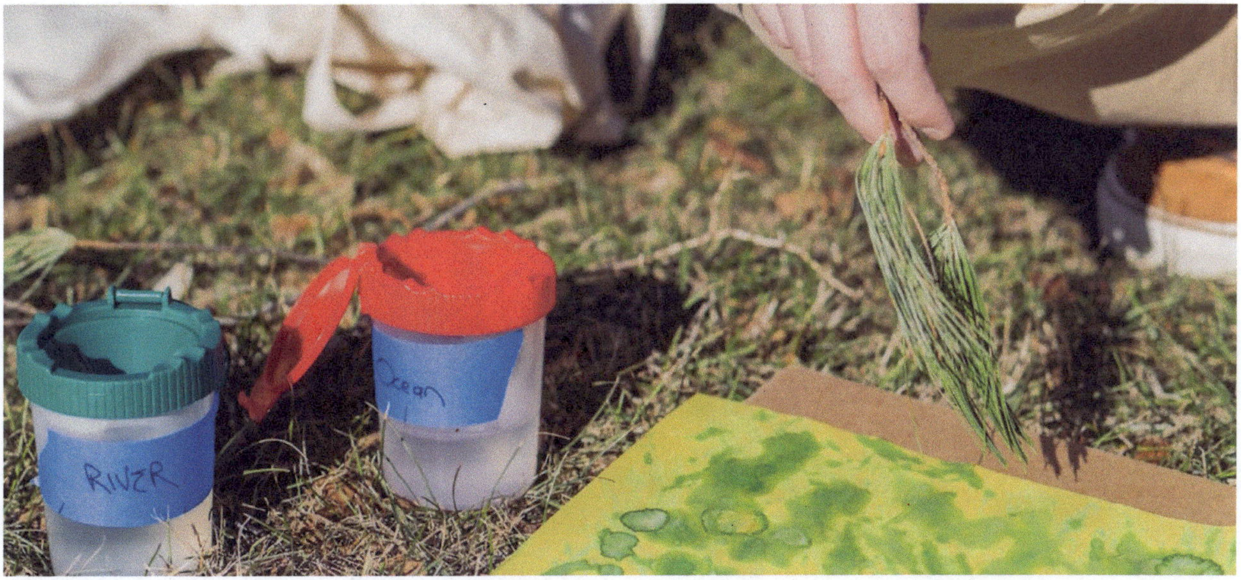

FIGURE 7.4 Evelyn Rydz, *The Mouth: A Merrimack River Project Workshop*, January 16, 2020. Photo: Mel Taing

A water cooler filled with hundreds of used hypodermic needles, contributed by Rocky Morrison, founder and director of the Methuen-based Clean River Project, was placed between Rydz and Yang's installations in the UMass Lowell gallery. Morrison and volunteers have pulled needles by the thousands from the river. The crisis of addiction and the course of the river are entwined. The Merrimack originates in the foothills of the White Mountains in central New Hampshire and flows through the state's largest cities—Concord, Manchester, and Nashua—before crossing into Massachusetts and flowing through Lowell, Lawrence, and Haverhill. In the nineteenth century, the river powered the Industrial Revolution. It now tracks the human geography of the opioid epidemic, a postindustrial crisis affecting the very communities built by the mills. Yang met Rocky Morrison during his research on the impact of plastics for *Local Ecologies*, inviting Morrison to show this sculpture as part of the exhibition. Yang calls the cooler "a powerful and evocative artifact of our complex socio-bio-ecology."[2]

Andrew S. Yang's zine for *Waste Knot, Want Knot* interrogates our complicated relationship to plastic and how waste impacts global waterways. A downloadable PDF that can be printed double-sided and folded in half can be found here: https://doi.org/10.3998/mpub.13189112.cmp.56

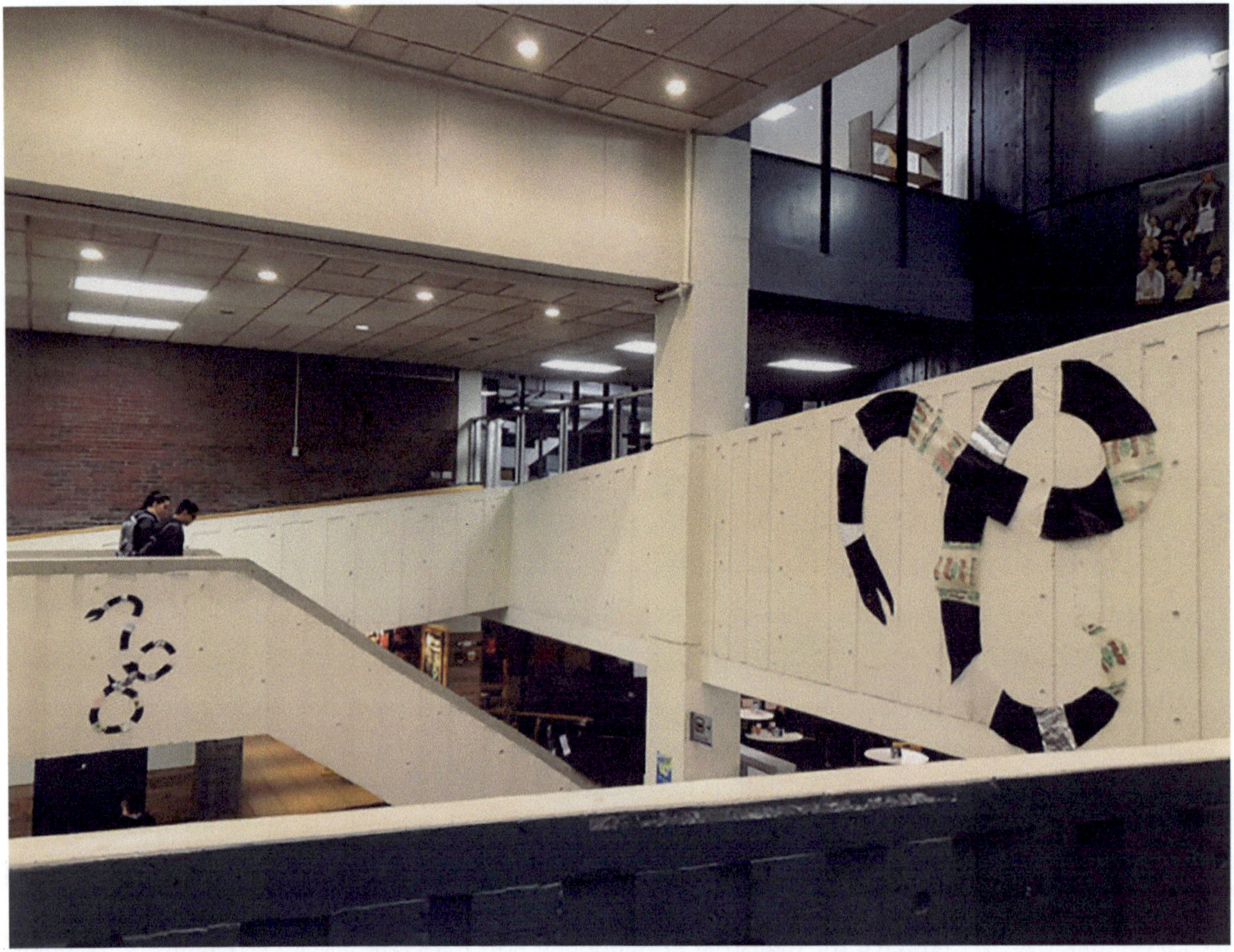

FIGURE 7.5 Andrew S. Yang, *Waste Knot, Want Knot*, February 2020, in situ. Photo: Andrew S. Yang

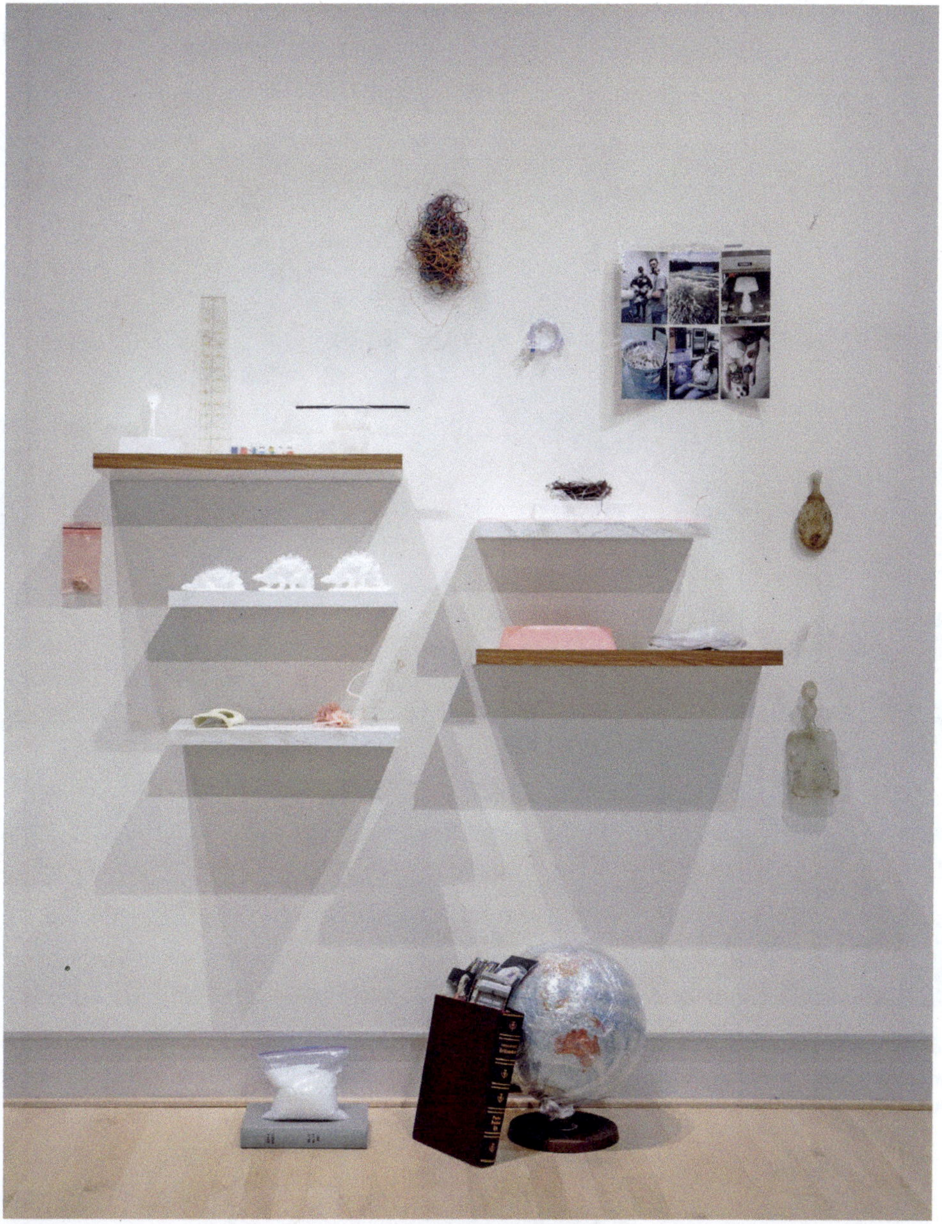

FIGURE 7.6 Andrew S. Yang, *Waste Knot, Want Knot*, 2020, gallery installation

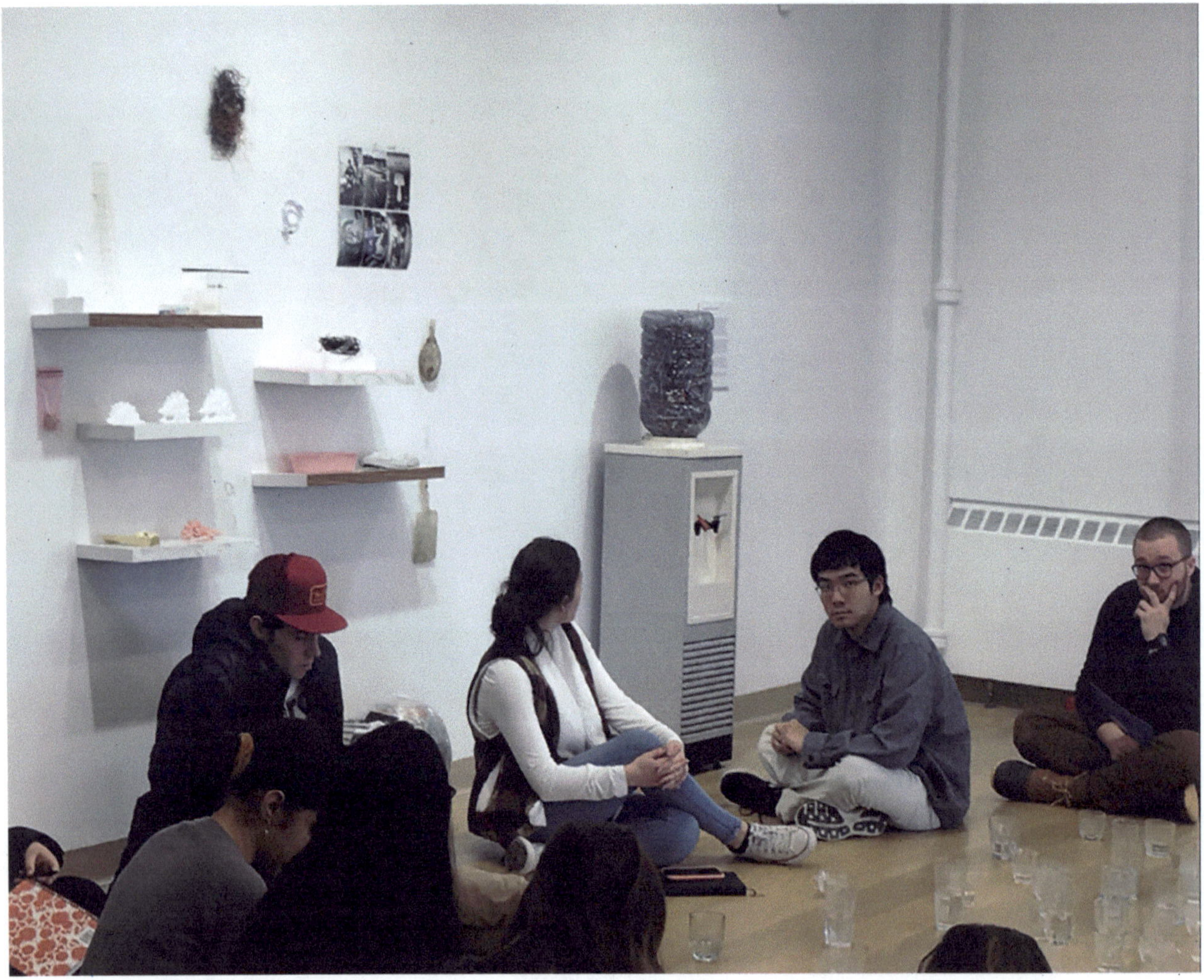

FIGURE 7.7 Andrew S. Yang, *Waste Knot, Want Knot* (forms of forming), 2020 (left). Clean River Project, *Untitled water cooler filled with used hypodermic needles found in the Merrimack River*, 2020 (right). Evelyn Rydz, *The Mouth: A Merrimack River Project*, 2019, foreground. Photo: Deborah Santoro

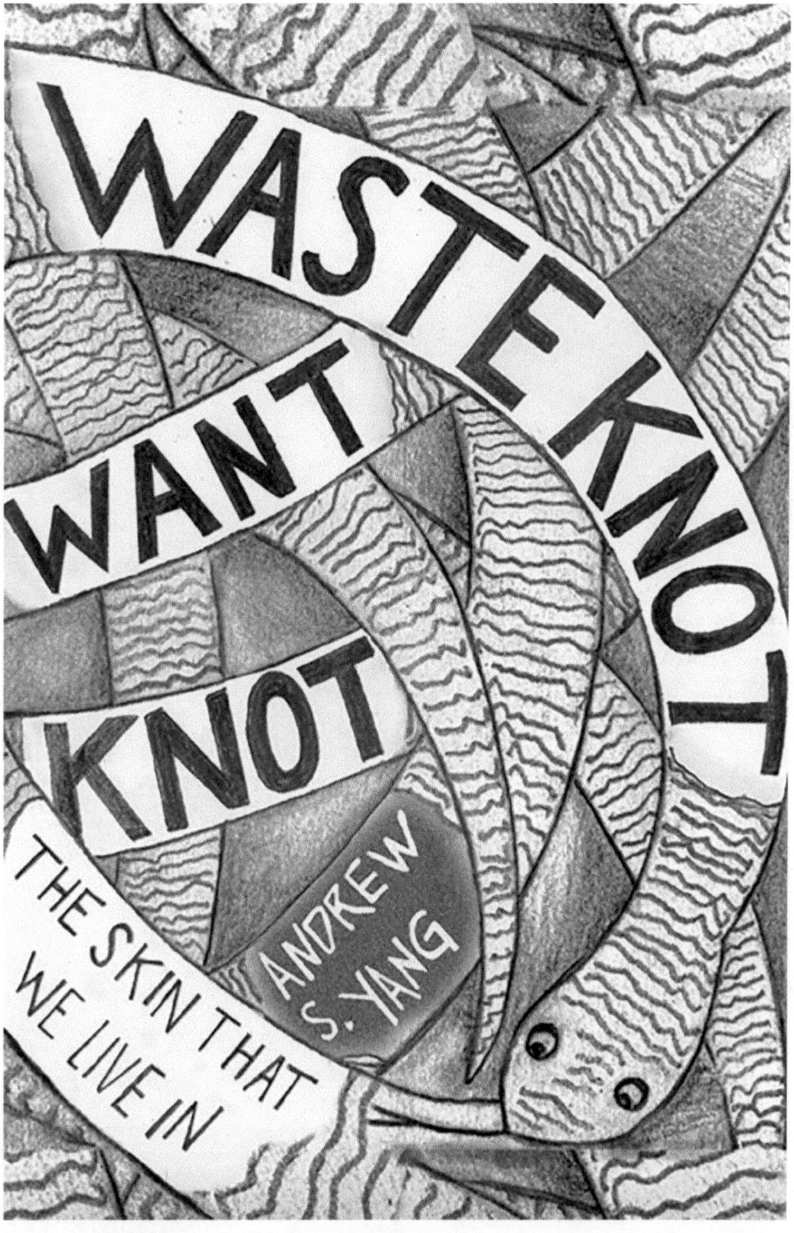

FIGURE 7.8 Cover of Andrew S. Yang's *Waste Knot, Want Knot*, 2020

CHAPTER 8
Coda: Dear Readers

A concluding letter to readers follows from the art collective Plotform, a partnership between Jane Marsching and Andi Sutton. Plotform offers an elegiac, optimistic, heartfelt entreatment to the readers of this volume—in a context of climate "weirdness" where it may be difficult to find or feel agency. Through a series of multimedia contributions, Plotform ends our volume with visions and sounds excerpted from their *Dear Harbor Radio* project of 2019.

The nature of this overall project is not definitive. Through this volume, in dialogue with offerings from many invited artists, cultural producers, activists, environmentalists, and interpreters, we hope to have illustrated and opened up many methodological approaches to the questions of how to address the multiplacedness of place within historical, cultural, and environmental contexts subject to rapid change and contradiction. *Dear Harbor Radio* signs us off from this exploration with sounds of a shortwave, nomadic radio broadcast featuring multiple participants: human, nonhuman, individual, and collective.

DEAR READERS

Jane Marsching and Andi Sutton

Dear readers,
Climate weirding, and the human and nonhuman losses and transformations associated with it, is ever more in the public consciousness. It's a staggering narrative of loss we are living through, ignoring, writing, and perpetuating, defined by the threatened, thinning, and breaking strands of the web of life. One can imagine these strands floating through the air, seeking reconnection, but missing it in the chaos of climate disruption. It's a super sad, true love story.

This poignant tale is also the very real and urgent situation we find ourselves in right now, and is the heart of the work of Plotform, a collective formed in 2012 by Jane D. Marsching and Andi Sutton. Our projects activate the interconnectedness of riparian and other species by scrambling strategies from ecological design, craftivism, public engagement, tactical urbanism, interspecies communication, micronations, and

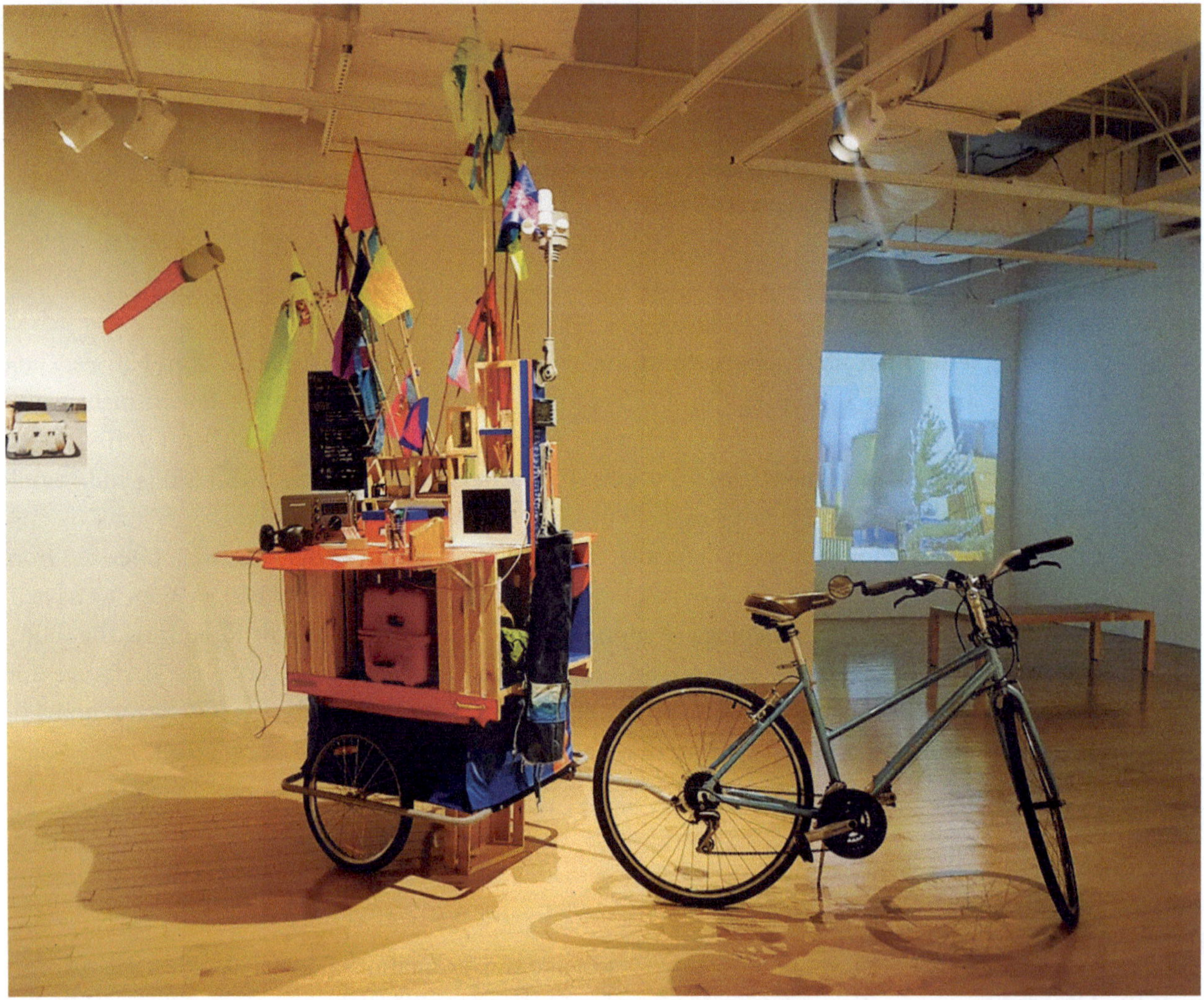

FIGURE 8.1 *Dear Harbor Radio,* installation shot

empathetic making. We want to create moving experiences of ecological interconnectedness that instigate individuals and communities to enact healing in their local ecologies.

Dear Harbor Radio is a participatory, roving, public installation that is at once a bike-pulled mobile radio station, a writing and recording studio, and a series of public interventions. The project was first sited in New Bedford, Massachusetts in 2019. It seeks to bring clarity, attention, and care to the broken relationships between humans and our many nonhuman neighbors in and far beyond New Bedford.

Dear Harbor Radio was commissioned in 2019 for the art exhibition *Local Ecologies*, which took place across three University of Massachusetts campuses: Boston, Dartmouth, and Lowell. *Dear Harbor Radio* launched as a site-specific piece in New Bedford, Massachusetts. However, from 2019 to 2020, through public performances and gallery exhibitions, it evolved to become what it is today: a performing object as well as a set of strategies that can be employed by anyone, anywhere, who is interested in reconnecting their lost or ruptured relationships with beloved members of the natural world.

We are delighted to introduce you to *Dear Harbor Radio* through this collection of documents and works. Here you will find the following:

1. *DEAR HARBOR RADIO BIKING THE HARBOR*, 2019

This video documents the travels of *Dear Harbor Radio* through various locations in Massachusetts harbors, from New Bedford to Boston, in 2019. It was displayed on the cart during all exhibitions, public events, and love-letter-writing gatherings.
https://doi.org/10.3998/mpub.13189112.cmp.58

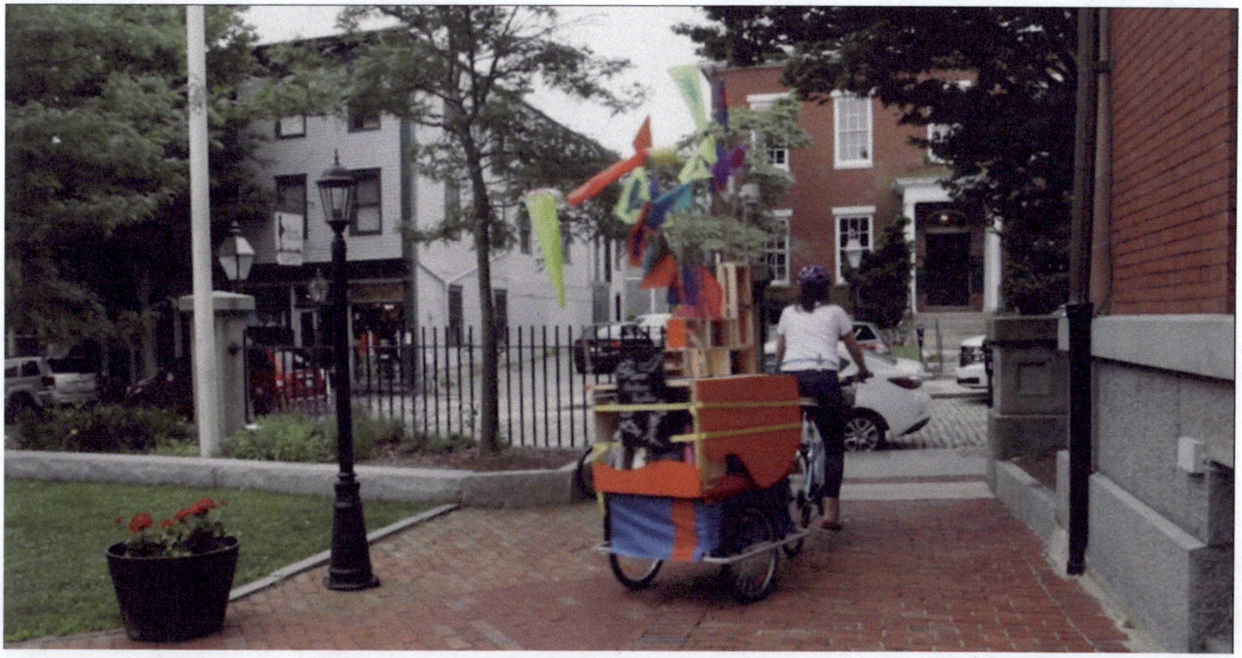

FIGURE 8.2 Still from Plotform "Biking the Harbor," 2019

2. *DEAR HARBOR RADIO* TRANSMISSION, 2019–2020

This sound file is a collection of all the love letters recorded with *Dear Harbor Radio*. You'll hear love expressed in a myriad of forms: letters, observations, recordings, songs, conversations—a series of calls of love from humans to other-than-humans and back again.
https://doi.org/10.3998/mpub.13189112.cmp.59

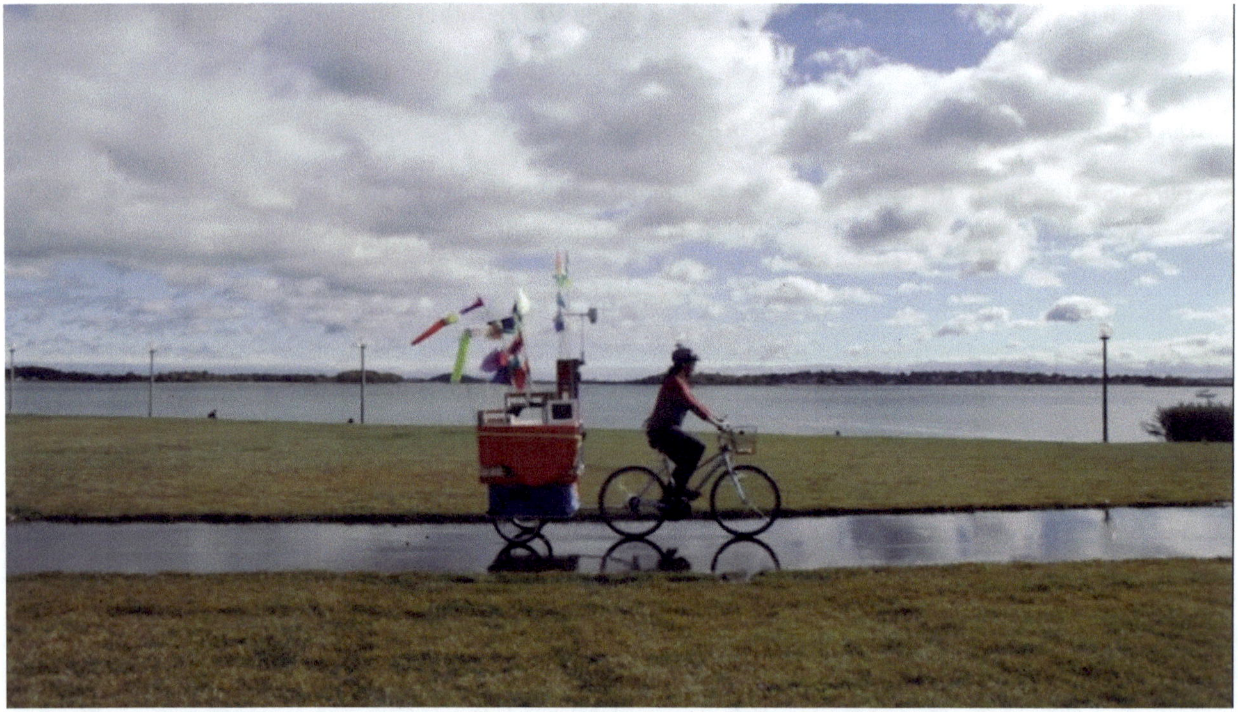

FIGURE 8.3 Still from Plotform "Biking the Harbor," 2019

3. RADIO BROADCAST PLAYLIST, 2021

A list of all the radio content included in the pirate broadcast.
https://doi.org/10.3998/mpub.13189112.cmp.60

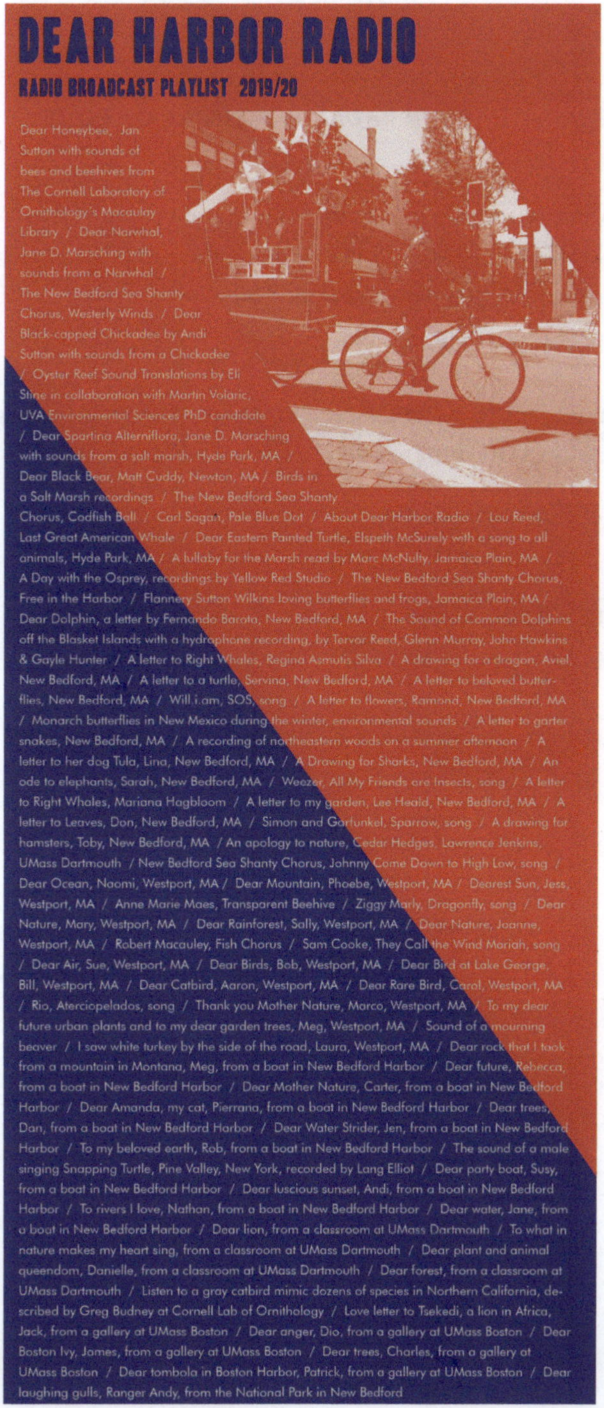

FIGURE 8.4 Plotform, "Dear Harbor Radio," 2021, broadside

4. THE LOVE LETTERS OF *DEAR HARBOR RADIO*: A MANUAL OF LOVE LETTERS FOR LOVE LETTER WRITING, 2021

> A compilation of the love letters written to guide others in the production of their own gatherings of *Dear Harbor Radio*, this book includes love letters written by Plotform to other-than-humans, to the participants in the letter writing workshops they produced as part of the piece, and more.
> https://doi.org/10.3998/mpub.13189112.cmp.61

We invite you to learn about and employ the strategies that we offer in these pages. May they help to reconnect some of the broken strands of the dynamic living web of which we humans are only a small part.

Sincerely,

Plotform (Jane D. Marsching + Andi Sutton)

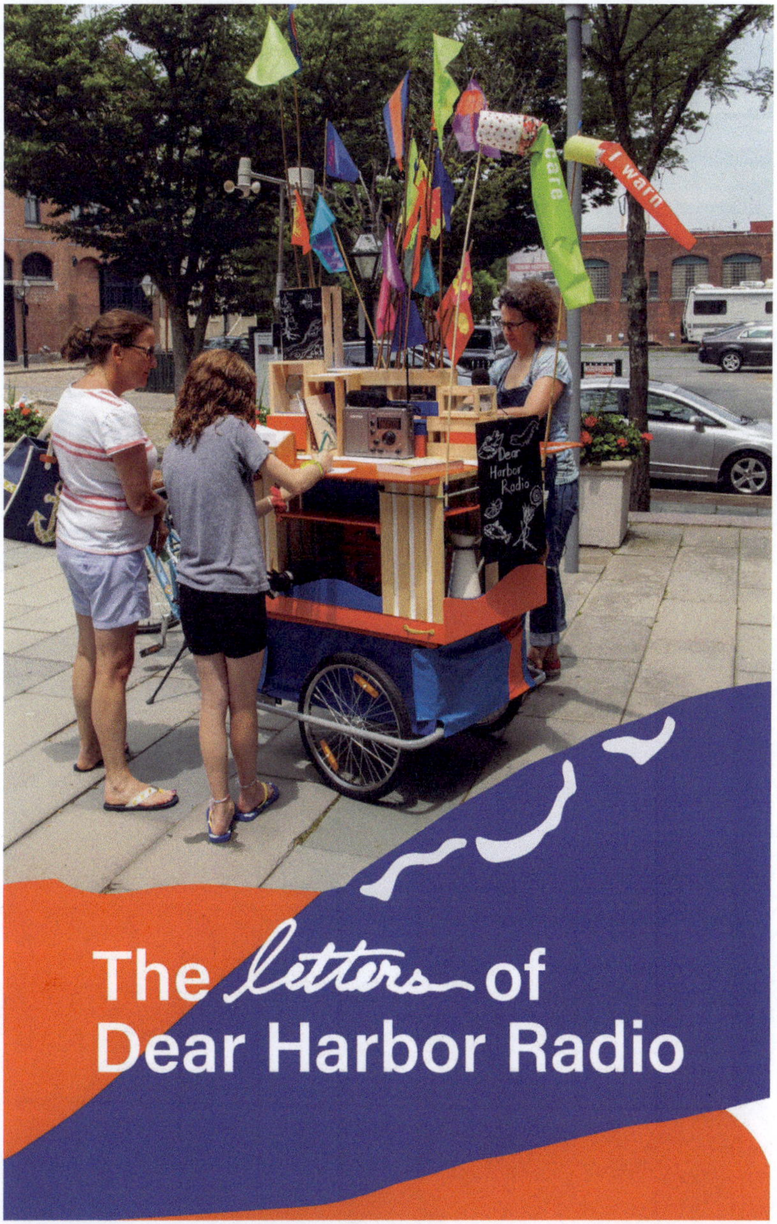

FIGURE 8.5 Plotform, *The Letters of Dear Harbor Radio*, 2021

Notes

Acknowledgments

1 "Restoring Truth and Sanity to American History," White House Presidential Executive Order, March 27, 2025. https://www.whitehouse.gov/presidential-actions/2025/03/restoring-truth-and-sanity-to-american-history/

Chapter 1: In the Absence of Cultural Reflections: Looking for a Landscape

1 "A Garden Grows at the MFA" (Summer 2021). https://www.mfa.org/exhibition/garden-for-boston/video/a-garden-grows-at-the-mfa. Elizabeth James-Perry was a collaborator in the UMass Dartmouth courses and events that occurred during the *Local Ecologies* exhibition and programs documented in this volume.

2 Lisa Lowe, *The Intimacies of Four Continents* (Durham, NC: Duke University Press, 2015), 2.

Chapter 2: Not Neutral Ground: Creative Landscapes of Eastern Massachusetts

1 City of Cambridge site marker installed at Jerry's Pond and available online. Environmental Protection Agency, "Site Investigation for the W.R. Grace Site" (August/September 2000). https://www.cambridgema.gov/-/media/Files/historicalcommission/pdf/markers_NC_jerryspit.pdf

2 Dan Borelli, "Bric-à-brac: a collaborative brick-making project for Jerry's Pit," project proposal for Cambridge Arts Center (2023).

3 By Cambridge city ordinance, 1 percent of the construction costs on municipal capital investment must be designated for use in developing site-responsive public artwork. https://www.cambridgema.gov/arts/publicart/percentforart

4 Dan Borelli, "Color Fields: A Pathway from Jerry's Pit to Mass Ave," project proposal for Cambridge Arts Council, 2023.

5 Henry David Thoreau, *Cape Cod* (Boston: Ticknor and Fields, 1865).

6 Cambridge Historical Commission, "Jerry's Pond" (2000). https://www.cambridgema.gov/-/media/Files/historicalcommission/pdf/markers_NC_jerryspit.pdf

7 Roy F. Weston, "Site Investigation Report for the W.R. Grace Site," prepared for US Environmental Protection Agency (August/September 2000). https://alewifeneighbors.org/reports/archive/epa_weston.pdf

8 Roy F. Weston, "Site Investigation Report for the W.R. Grace Site," prepared for US Environmental Protection Agency (August/September 2000). https://alewifeneighbors.org/reports/archive/epa_weston.pdf

9 "IQHQ Inc," business profile, *Bloomberg*. https://www.bloomberg.com/profile/company/1784632D:US

10 Hannah Chanatry, "A Polluted Pond in Cambridge is Poised for Cleanup – But Its Future Is Under Debate," *WBUR*, December 18, 2020. https://www.wbur.org/news/2020/12/18/jerrys-pond-cambridge-cleanup-future. See also Joyce Doherty, "With New Owner Comes New Hope for Jerry's Pond in Cambridge," *Wicked Local*, December 17, 2020. https://www.wickedlocal.com/story/cambridge-chronicle-tab/2020/12/17/with-new-owner-comes-new-hope-for-jerrys-pond-in-cambridge/3945764001/

11 Letter to Cambridge City Council from O. Robert Simha, MIT Planning Director, 1960–2000 (July 5, 2019). Letter included on website Cambridgecitizens.org now deleted. Archived at https://web.archive.org/web/20210309124959/https://www.cccoalition.org/blog/the-deeply-flawed-city-wide-up-zoning-plan-letter-to-cambridge-city-council-from-o-robert-simha-mits-planning-director-1960-2000?fbclid=IwAR2lmiQDQGrLPfL_11VSL1FbtQ4t9jAI3B9c4mC-OjfRn-kPH-aVzsdaufg

12 "Alewife Revitalization: Urban Design Study Phase II," p. iv. City of Cambridge Community Development Department, 1979. https://www.cambridgema.gov/~/media/Files/CDD/Planning/Studies/Alewife/alewife_fishbook_1979.pdf

13 The authors would like to thank Cambridge resident and activist Eric Grunebaum for sharing insights and factual knowledge regarding Jerry's Pond, Rindge Towers, and Danehy Park.

14 Mierle Laderman Ukeles, "A Journey: Earth/City/Flow," *Art Journal* 51 no. 2 (Summer 1992), 12.

15 Hafthor Yngvason, ed. *Conservation and Maintenance of Contemporary Public Art* (Cambridge: Cambridge Arts Council, 2002), 11.

16 Mierle Laderman Ukeles/Danehy Park records in Cambridge Arts Council Archives.

17 Mierle Laderman Ukeles/Danehy Park records in Cambridge Arts Council Archives.

18 Mierle Laderman Ukeles/Danehy Park records in Cambridge Arts Council Archives.

19 "North Cambridge Neighborhood Study," City of Cambridge Community Development Department, 1990, 13.

20 Jill Sinclair, *Fresh Pond: The History of a Cambridge Landscape* (Cambridge, MA: MIT Press, 2009), 46.

21 Henry David Thoreau, "Where I Live and What I Lived For," in *Walden; or, Life in the Woods* (London: J.M. Dent, 1908).

22 Ralph Waldo Emerson, *Nature* (Boston: James Munroe and Company, 1849), 1.

23 "Walden Pond Visitor Center Project," Mass.gov. https://www.mass.gov/service-details/walden-pond-visitor-center-project

24 Alison Flood, "Pee and Pesticides: Thoreau's Walden Pond in Trouble, Warn Scientists," *The Guardian*, April 6, 2018. https://www.theguardian.com/books/2018/apr/06/pee-and-pesticides-henry-david-thoreau-walden-pond-in-trouble-warn-scientists

25 Dina Deitsch, "Floating Cabins and Shifting Landscapes: William Lamson in Conversation with Dina Deitsch," *Art Journal Open*, April 9, 2015. http://artjournal.collegeart.org/?p=5998

26 J. Morgan Puett and Mark Dion, organized at the Tufts University Aidekman Arts Center in 2010 by the collaborative pair curatorsquared—Ginger Gregg Duggan and Judith Hoos Fox.

27 Gilbert E. Metcalf, "An Economist's Perspective on Walden" in *Mildred's Lane: Renovating Walden*, ed. Mark Dion and J. Morgan Puett/Mildred's Lane and the Trustees of Tufts College (Medford, MA: Tufts University Arts Gallery, 2010), 10.

28 Henry David Thoreau, "Economy," in *Walden; or, Life in the Woods* (London: J.M. Dent, 1908).

29 Caitlin O'Keefe and Asma Khalid, "Remembering The Forgotten People Of Walden," *WBUR*, July 12, 2017. https://www.wbur.org/radioboston/2017/07/12/walden-thoreau-forgotten

30 Elise Lemire, *Black Walden: Slavery and its Aftermath in Concord, Massachusetts* (Philadelphia: University of Pennsylvania Press, 2009), 170, 152.

31 William M. Denevan, "The Pristine Myth: The Landscape of the Americas in 1492," *Annals of the Association of American Geographers* 82, no. 3 (1992), 369–85. http://www.jstor.org/stable/2563351. Denevin notes that Thoreau believed that "New England forests of 1633 were more open, more park-like, with more berries and more wildlife, than Thoreau observed in 1855," acknowledging that "a strong case can be made for significant environmental recovery and reduction of cultural features by the late eighteenth century as a result of Indian population decline" (378).

32 Arjun Appadurai, "Putting Hierarchy in its Place," *Cultural Anthropology* 3, no. 1 (1988): 36–49.

33 Appadurai, "Putting Hierarchy in its Place," 1988

34 Nearly 100 years ago, Robert Musil wrote that "there is nothing in this world as invisible as a monument," reminding us how the naturalization of history transpires through its resolution as a status-quo, background given. More recently, Kirk Savage asserted, "A funny thing happened once a monument was built and took its place in the landscape of people's lives: it became a natural fact, as if it had always been meant to be.... Public monuments exercised a curious power to erase their own political origins and become sacrosanct." Robert Musil, "Monuments," in *Posthumous Papers of a Living Author* (Hygiene, Colorado: Eridanos Press, 1987), 61. Kirk Savage, *Standing Soldiers, Kneeling Slaves: Race, War, and Monument in Nineteenth-Century America* (Princeton, NJ and Oxford: Princeton University Press, 2018), 7.

35 https://art21.org/watch/art-in-the-twenty-first-century/s3/krzysztof-wodiczko-in-power-segment/

36 See David Eltis and David Richardson, eds. *Atlas of the Transatlantic Slave Trade* (New Haven: Yale University Press, 2010).

37 Steve Locke, "Why I withdrew my proposed slave memorial at Faneuil Hall," *Boston Globe*, August 4, 2019. https://www.bostonglobe.com/opinion/2019/08/05/why-withdrew-proposed-slave-memorial-faneuil-hall/cNblyYuH2xVxsVuCvbDgFP/story.html. An interesting comparison to this project can be seen in the artwork and memorial at Baltimore's Lexington Market by Oletha DeVane and Christopher Kojar. *Robert and Rosetta*, installed in late 2022 at the Lexington Market, commemorates two individuals known to be connected to the market through 1830s print culture: a runaway notice describing Robert that ran in *The Baltimore American and Commercial Daily Advertiser* and a sale advertisement promoting an auction for Rosetta's continued enslavement in the *Baltimore Sun*. In addition to the colorful Figurative gateway sculpture showing two people in profile, the artwork includes these two notices engraved in granite and set into the ground below as a direct linkage to the history of Robert and Rosetta and the market to which their stories were connected. https://www.baltimoresun.com/features/newsmaker/bs-fe-newsmaker-oletha-devane-artist-lexington-market-20221108-fcr23x4o5nhovmxet2a5rnkoo4-story.html

38 "Please read: Important Changes to Project," July 16, 2019, email communication posted by Steve Locke on the *Auction Block Memorial at Faneuil Hall* Kickstarter page. https://www.kickstarter.com/projects/auctionblockmemorial/auction-block-memorial/posts/2567522

39 Locke, "Please read: Important Changes to Project."

40 Eve Tuck, "Suspending Damage: A Letter to Communities," *Harvard Educational Review* 79, no. 3 (2009), 411–412.

41 Sarah Lewis, "Groundwork: Race and Aesthetics in an Era of Stand Your Ground Law," *Art Journal* 79, no. 4 (2020), 111.

42 Rebecca Uchill, interview with Alex Criqui and Dustin Klein. February 22, 2021.

43 Yvonne Abraham, "Trust and Transformation in a Roxbury Neighborhood," *Boston Globe*, July 24, 2014. https://www.bostonglobe.com/metro/2014/07/23/roxbury-neighborhood-once-monument-racism-and-neglect-undergoes-transformation/QcWotBYJZYGoZD3OU4u0lO/story.html

44 Ekua Holmes, "Roxbury Sunflower Project," personal website. https://www.ekuaholmes.com/public-engagement/roxbury-sunflower-project

45 Boston Associated Press, "Boston Museum of Fine Arts Acts over Middle Schoolers' Racism Claim," *The Guardian*, May 25, 2019. https://www.theguardian.com/us-news/2019/may/25/boston-museum-of-fine-arts-middle-school-racism

46 Murray Whyte, "Planting Seeds of Change at the MFA," *Boston Globe*, August 19, 2021.

47 Interview with Kenneth Bailey and Rebecca K. Uchill, August 21, 2023.

48 Interview with Kenneth Bailey and Rebecca K. Uchill, August 21, 2023.

49 María Magdelena Campos-Pons in conversation with Dan Borelli and Andrew Schnetzer, moderated by Rebecca Uchill. Zoom recording, March 15, 2021 [note: lightly edited].

50 https://www.nps.gov/planyourvisit/event-details.htm?id=288829F3-A610-46A4-0074A8381B359AA6

Chapter 3: Introduction: Local Ecologies

1 This introduction is adapted from Kirsten Swenson and Rebecca Uchill, "Local Ecologies," *Boston Art Review* 5 (Summer 2020).

2 John D. Kelly, "New Bedford, Capital of the 19th Century?" *Anthropological Quarterly* 90, no. 4 (Fall 2017), 1085–1126.

3 For an overview of Benjamin's text, as well as a related interpretive riff, see Derek Sayer, "Introduction," in *Prague, Capital of the Twentieth Century: A Surrealist History* (Princeton, NJ and Oxford: Princeton University Press, 2013).

4 Peter Galison and Caroline A. Jones, "Unknown Quantities," *Artforum* (November 2010): 49–50.

Chapter 4: Ecologies of Acknowledgment

1 Quote from the label that accompanied the installation, which was developed with the artists.

2 Quote from the label that accompanied the installation, which was developed with the artists.

Chapter 5: Botanies of Migration

1 Email to the author from UMass Lowell Director of Campus Planning and Development, April 30, 2019.

2 Email to the author from UMass Lowell Director of Campus Planning and Development, April 30, 2019.

3 "Pollinator Gardens," UMass Lowell. https://web.archive.org/web/20230928142655/https://www.uml.edu/office-sustainability/practices/grounds/pollinator-gardens.aspx

4 "South Campus Landscape Plan," UMass Lowell. https://www.uml.edu/office-sustainability/Practices/Grounds/South-Campus-Landscape-Plan.aspx

5 "UMass Lowell South Campus Master Plan," Crosby | Schlessinger | Smallridge, LLC. http://www.cssboston.com/portfolio/umass-lowell-south-campus-master-plan/

Chapter 6: Ground Truthing

1 For more information about New Bedford Harbor's history of pollution and ongoing cleanup, see the Boston University School of Public Health Superfund Research Program at https://www.bu.edu/sph/about/departments/environmental-health/research/superfund-research-program-at-boston-university/research-cores/community-engagement-core/new-bedford-harbor/

2 See Dan Borelli's artist book *The Whiteness of the Whale* at https://doi.org/10.3998/mpub.13189112.cmp.48

3 We acknowledge here the tremendous efforts of gallery director Viera Levitt, who tirelessly sourced the planks and molasses for this installation work and in every way acted as a supportive curatorial collaborator for the UMass Dartmouth campus presentation of *Local Ecologies.*

Chapter 7: Life of the Merrimack

1 Henry David Thoreau, "A Week on the Merrimack and Concord Rivers," in *The Writings of Henry David Thoreau* (Boston: Houghton and Mifflin, 1906), 32.

2 Andrew S. Yang quoted on wall label for Rocky Morrison, *Local Ecologies* exhibition.

Contributor Biographies

Kenneth Bailey is the co-founder of the Design Studio for Social Intervention (DS4SI). His interests focus on the research and development of design tools for marginalized communities to address complex social issues. Projects he has produced at DS4SI include Action Lab, Public Kitchen, Social Emergency Response Center (SERC), People's Redevelopment Authority, and inPUBLIC. Bailey was a Visiting Scholar in collaboration with University of Tasmania and also a founding member of Theatrum Mundi NYC with Richard Sennett. His book (coauthored with DS4SI) is entitled *Ideas Arrangements Effects: Systems Design and Social Justice* (Minor Compositions, 2020). He received his MFA in Public Action from Bennington College in 2021.

Lauren Berlin is a PhD candidate in Musicology at the University of Rochester whose research explores the development of American identity on the postwar TV variety show. Berlin's research has been supported by awards and fellowships from the Society for American Music, the Mellon Foundation, the Eastman School of Music, the University of Rochester, and the Susan B. Anthony Institute for Gender, Sexuality and Women's Studies. Her writing appears in *PopMatters* and the *Oxford Handbook of Music and Television.*

Dan Borelli is an artist and Director of Exhibitions at Harvard University, Graduate School of Design (GSD). His art practice focuses on environmental justice, contaminated communities, and how research-based art can address shared traumas. His current project, "Unfriending the Atom," started in 2021 and is an ongoing collaboration with the scientist Marco Kaltofen. His long-range and socially engaged artwork "Illuminating Futures: Ashland and Nyanza" makes public hidden narratives of cancer clusters, human loss, activism, and ultimately regeneration surrounding one of the first Superfund sites in the United States, and received funding from ArtPlace America, the National Endowment of the Arts, Harvard's Initiative in Learning Technology, and an ongoing collaboration with the Laborers Union New England Training Academy.

Nicholas A. Brown is a teacher, writer, artist, and walker based in Boston, Massachusetts and La Farge, Wisconsin. He teaches in the School of Architecture and Department of History at Northeastern University in Boston. Brown's scholarly and creative work focuses on Indigenous and settler-colonial landscapes. He is the coauthor of

Re-Collecting Black Hawk: Landscape, Memory, and Power in the American Midwest and is currently working on a book about the Pacific Crest Trail.

María Magdalena Campos-Pons, born in 1959 in La Vega, Cuba, grew up on a sugar plantation in a family of Nigerian, Hispanic, and Chinese heritage. Her multicultural background deeply informs her autobiographical art, which explores identity through history, memory, gender, and religion using photography, performance, painting, sculpture, film, and video. Her work often references the Transatlantic slave trade, plantation life, and Afro-Cuban religious practices.

In the late 1980s, she taught at Havana's Instituto Superior de Arte and became a key figure in the New Cuban Art movement. She moved to Boston in 1991 and has exhibited internationally, including at MoMA, the National Gallery of Canada, and the Smithsonian. She has performed globally and participated in major art events like the Venice Biennale and Documenta. In 2017, she was appointed to the Cornelius Vanderbilt Chair at Vanderbilt University. In 2023, she was awarded the title of MacArthur Foundation Fellow. Her work is held in over 30 major museum collections worldwide.

Padmini Chandrasekaran is a graphic designer, artist, and educator based in Lowell, MA. She received her BFA in Communication Design from Parsons, The New School for Design and an MFA in Graphic Design from Boston University. Her creative practice combines graphical image-making and data visualization with storytelling that speaks to themes related to belonging, insecurities, and personal connections. Aside from being an Associate Teaching Professor of Graphic Design at the University of Massachusetts Lowell, she is a member of an exhibiting artist collaborative, Radius Collective.

Duy Hoàng is an interdisciplinary artist born in Vietnam in 1989 and is currently residing in New York City. His work focuses on transitional spaces and the symbiotic relationships, conversing in the web of reciprocity. He received a BFA from the University of Massachusetts Lowell and an MFA from Columbia University. Hoàng has exhibited across the United States and internationally, including at Festival Images Vevey in Switzerland; Museum of Contemporary Art Vojvodina, Serbia; South Dakota State University; Kleine Humboldt Galerie in Berlin; ICA Singapore; Thomas Erben Gallery in New York; Lorber Family Gallery in Israel; the Royal Geographical Society Pavilion, London; and Cahoon Museum of American Art, Massachusetts. Hoàng is currently Expanded Media Professor at Alfred University.

Sarah Kanouse is an interdisciplinary artist and writer whose work explores the politics of landscape and space through video, photography, and performance. Her research-based projects uncover hidden stories of environmental and social change. A frequent collaborator, she has worked with Ryan Griffis and Nicholas Brown on *Anthropocene Drift* for *Mississippi: An Anthropocene River*, and co-founded the National Toxic Land/Labor Conservation Service with Shiloh Krupar to address the cultural and ecological effects of nuclear militarism. Her work has been shown at venues like Documenta 13, Haus der Kulturen der Welt, MCA Chicago, Cooper Union, and various universities. She has published in *Art Journal*, *Parallax*, and other journals and edited volumes on environmental art. She is Associate Professor of Creative Media at Northeastern University.

Jane Marsching's work creates spaces for wonder, kinship with more-than-human beings, and urgent ecological reflection. Her practice thrives on intimate, often unpredictable collaborations that emerge from a deep engagement with place—whether a city park, observatory, science lab, or rooftop. Her work has been shown at Northern Spark (Minneapolis), Kilroy Metal Ceiling (Brooklyn), Galerie Lucy Mackintosh (Switzerland), Tierra des Explorades (Buenos Aires), and MassMoCA. She has received support from Creative Capital and Artadia, among others. She coedited *Far Field: Digital Culture, Climate Change, and the Poles* with Andrea Polli (Intellect, 2012). Marsching co-founded Platform2: Art and Activism (2009–2012), and from 2013 to 2020 collaborated with Andi Sutton and others in the collective Plotform on projects focused on climate, citizen science, and water ecologies. She is Professor and Sustainability Fellow at Massachusetts College of Art and Design.

Matthew Mazzotta works at the intersection of art, activism, and urbanism, focusing on the power of the built environment to shape our relationships and experiences. Matthew's public art projects have received international art and architecture awards such as the Architizer A+ Award, Azure's AZ Award, CODAawards, WAN Award, and Americans for the Arts. His work has been featured on CNN, BBC, NPR, The Colbert Report, and Discovery Channel, published in numerous books, journals, and magazines, and featured in exhibitions including the19th International Architecture Exhibition of the Venice Bienniale. Mazzotta received his BFA degree from the School of the Art Institute of Chicago and his Master of Science from the Massachusetts Institute of Technology's Program in Art, Culture, and Technology. He is a TED Fellow, a Guggenheim Fellow, a Fulbright Grantee, and a Smithsonian Artist in Research, as well as a Loeb Fellow at Harvard University.

Evelyn Rydz works across drawing, site-responsive installations, and community projects to reimagine our relationships with the natural world and with each other. Her practice explores connections between bodies of water, personal histories, consumer cycles, and threats to natural and cultural ecosystems. Rydz has received grants from Artadia, Joan Mitchell Foundation, U.S. Latinx Art Forum, Brother Thomas Fund, and Mass Cultural Council. Exhibitions include features at Harvard Radcliffe Institute, Cambridge, MA; Anchorage Museum, AK; Lowe Art Museum, Miami, FL; MFA, Boston, MA; Palacio de Justicia, Matanzas, Cuba. Her community-based work includes projects for the University of Massachusetts, ICA Watershed, Boston University, Ethelbert Cooper Gallery of African & African American Art, and MIT List Visual Arts Center.

Andy Schnetzer is a National Park Service ranger specializing in education and community engagement. The goals of his work at Roger Williams National Memorial are to promote understanding, foster kindness, and encourage curiosity. Schnetzer was a key participant in the establishment of the New Bedford Whaling National Historical Park artist residency program, and was described by the *Herald News* as "a bridge between the park and the larger arts and culture community."

Andi Sutton is Executive Director of the Southeast Regional Sustainable Development Partnership at the University of Minnesota Extension. She is also an artist whose practice, for decades rooted in Boston, MA, explores the ways that performance art methodology can create new models for community development and social change. Working in a solo and collective context her projects incorporate food, agriculture and the natural world, television and street intervention, video, performance, and installation. She co-led the social practice collective the National Bitter Melon Council (2004–2014), was a collaborating artist with Platform2: Art and Activism (2009–2012), and, with Jane D. Marsching, co-led the collective Plotform producing public, participatory projects focused on ecology and the climate emergency (2013–2020). Her works have been shown internationally at the Boston Center for the Arts), The Western Front, (Vancouver, BC), Los Angeles County Museum of Art (LACMA), the Yerba Buena Center for the Arts (San Francisco), the Yogyajarta New Media Art Laboratory (Yogyajarta, Indonesia), the SMART Museum (Chicago), Universidad Nacional (Bogotá, Colombia), the Anthology Film Archives (New York), and the Frederick R. Weisman Art Museum (Minneapolis, MN), among others.

Kirsten Swenson is Associate Professor of Art History at the University of Massachusetts, Lowell. She is the author of *Irrational Judgments: Eva Hesse, Sol LeWitt, and 1960s New York* (Yale University Press, 2015) and, with Emily Eliza Scott, coeditor and author of the volume *Critical Landscapes: Art, Space, Politics* (University of California Press, 2015). *Reclamations: Earthworks, Public Works, Environments*, a book she is writing on artist-designed landscapes, land reclamation, and urban redevelopment, has been supported by an American Council of Learned Societies Burkhardt Fellowship at the Kluge Center of the Library of Congress, and by research grants from the Graham Foundation and the Getty Research Institute.

Sam Toabe is a curator, artist, art historian, and educator based in Somerville, MA. They are the Gallery Director at the University Hall Gallery for the Art and Art History department at UMass Boston, as well as the director of Arts on the Point. Their practices focus on alternative curatorial approaches across a variety of periods and geographies, noncanonical art histories, and the advancement of cultural plurality throughout our global visual lexicons. Toabe holds a BFA from the Studio for Interrelated Media & Art History at MassArt, where they now serve as visiting graduate faculty, and an MA in History of Art and Museum Studies from Boston University.

Rebecca Uchill is Director of the Center for Art, Design, and Visual Culture at UMBC (CADVC). She studies modern and contemporary art and historiography of art institutions and epistemes in the twentieth and twenty-first centuries. Uchill earned her BA in Individualized Studies at the Gallatin School for Individualized Study at NYU, her MA in art history at Williams College, and her PhD in History, Theory, and Criticism of Art and Architecture at MIT, where she later served as visiting faculty and postdoctoral fellow in the Center for Art, Science, and Technology. She has held curatorial positions at institutions including Mass MoCA, the Indianapolis Museum of Art, and the Carpenter Center for the Visual Arts at Harvard University.

Andrew S. Yang works across the visual arts and natural sciences to explore our ecological entanglements. His projects have been exhibited from Oklahoma to Yokohama, including the 14th Istanbul Biennial, the Museum of Contemporary Art Chicago, the Smithsonian Museum of Natural History, and the Chicago Botanic Garden, with recent curatorial projects *Earthly Observatory* at SAIC Galleries and *Making Kin—Worlds Becoming* for the Center for Humans and Nature. His essays appear in journals like *Leonardo, Art Journal, the Journal of Visual Art Practice,* and books such as the *Routledge Handbook of Art, Science, and Technology Studies* and the series *Kinship: Belonging in a World of Relations.*